Watergate

WATERGATE
An Annotated Bibliography

Kenyon C. Rosenberg
and
Judith K. Rosenberg

LIBRARIES UNLIMITED, INC. Littleton, Colo.
1975

LIBRARIES UNLIMITED, INC.
P.O. Box 263
Littleton, Colorado 80120

Rosenberg, Kenyon C
    Watergate : an annotated bibliography.

    Includes indexes.
    1. Watergate Affair, 1972–   --Bibliography.
I. Rosenberg, Judith K., joint author. II. Title.
Z1245.R6 [E860] 016.3641'32   75-6880
ISBN 0-87287-116-9

Dedicated, with pleasure,
to the tertium quid—*Dana Rebecca*

TABLE OF CONTENTS

PREFACE

Despite its somewhat ludicrous beginning, the Watergate Affair has reached such proportions as to affect the interest of all segments of society. The proliferation of articles, newspaper editorials, and books on Watergate makes it extremely difficult for scholars, teachers, and librarians who must deal with these materials to choose the ones appropriate to their areas of research without combing through much that is inapplicable to their needs. If researchers had a single reference source that described the contents of these materials, they could better select what is relevant to their fields of inquiry. Such is the purpose of this bibliography.

Included here are all articles on Watergate to be found in the general interest magazines indexed in *The Reader's Guide to Periodical Literature* (excepting specialized periodicals such as *Aviation Week, Christianity Today,* and *Senior Scholastic*) and many that are not indexed therein; selected major editorials from eight outstanding American newspapers; pertinent articles from American law reviews; and a few books selected because of their high quality and their potential durability.

To facilitate tracing the factual developments, legal occurrences, and changes in public opinion as the case evolved, a chronological arrangement (by year, month and day of appearance) has been used. Articles and editorials appearing on the same day are listed by name of magazine, review, or newspaper, with title, author (if any), and pagination following. Brief descriptive annotations follow; entries that contain repetitive material are simply listed, and a "see" reference leads the user to the appropriate article previously annotated. Books are listed first under each year, followed by the chronologically arranged articles. Entries are numbered sequentially.

A complete list of the magazines, law reviews, and newspapers included in this bibliography may be found in the front of the book, while a list of books unavailable for examination but of potential interest is at the end. Appended are author, title, and subject and personal name indexes, which use the sequential numbers from the main body of the work to refer the user to the appropriate entry. Materials included were published between late June 1972 and August 1974, one week after former President Nixon resigned from office.

There are, of course, many Watergate-related topics, such as the ITT, milk, grain, Vesco, and Ellsberg cases, but the articles on these would fill another bibliography. *This bibliography is limited to those materials dealing specifically and*

9

primarily with Watergate, but the user should be aware of these related areas, and might want to refer to the subject index for a listing of the topics and personalities that might be of further research interest.

The authors wish to thank Susan Jenkins, Margaret Barnetson, and Janet Fritz for their invaluable research assistance, and typist Irene Radabaugh for her unending diligence.

Kenyon C. Rosenberg
Judith K. Rosenberg
December 1974

MAGAZINES AND JOURNALS INDEXED

Albany Law Review
America
American Bar Association Journal
American Scholar
Association of the Bar of the City of New York Record
Atlantic
Business Week
California Bar Journal
Case and Comment
Chicago Tribune
Christian Century
Christian Science Monitor
Commentary
Commonweal
Current
Denver Post
Discussion
Ebony
Esquire
Federal Communications Bar Journal
Fortune
Harper's
Harvard Journal on Legislation
International Socialist Review
Life
Los Angeles Times
Loyola Law Review
Nation
National Review
New Leader
New Republic
New York Magazine
New York Times
New York Times Magazine
New Yorker
Newsday

WATERGATE
An Annotated Bibliography

JUNE 1972

1   June 20, 1972—**Denver Post.**
    Humorously suggests Republicans need security to protect themselves from friends rather than Democrats. Lawrence O'Brien may be anxious to find who's behind Watergate, but whoever is did the Democrats a big favor.

2   June 20, 1972—**St. Louis Post-Dispatch.**
    Doubts whether FBI investigation will be complete, considering their own heavy reliance on electronic eavesdropping.

3   June 21, 1972—**Washington Post.**
    Compares Watergate break-in and post-arrest actions with "Mission Impossible" TV show. Hopes Republican Administration will thoroughly investigate and not leave it to the Democratic lawsuit to unearth the facts.

4   June 22, 1972—**Chicago Tribune.**
    Deplores Lawrence O'Brien's anti-Republican allegations as unproven gutter politics and guilt by association tactics.

5   June 22, 1972—**New York Times.**
    Calls for thorough Federal investigation.

JULY 1972

6   July 3, 1972—**Newsweek,** "Operation Watergate," pp. 18-21.
    A brief biography of those involved. Summarizes the initial break-in with Bernard Barker, E. Howard Hunt, and Charles Colson linked. Possible reasons for break-in might be replacing a bad bug, information search, or Cuban extremist plot.

7   July 3, 1972—**Time,** "Bugs at the Watergate: Bugging of Democratic National Committee Offices," pp. 10-11.
    Briefly describes events leading to discovery of the burglary, identifies the men directly involved, and links them tentatively to CREEP via James McCord and Bernard Baker, and to the White House via Charles Colson and E. Howard Hunt. Democrats' $1-million damage suit began at this time.

8   July 5, 1972–**Christian Century**, "GOP's Second Rate Caper," p. 763.
     Editorial condemning Ron Ziegler's refusal to comment on the burglary
because "I don't comment on things that are taken to lower-level district courts."

9   July 10, 1972–**Nation**, "Mafia Metaphor," Carey McWilliams, pp. 2-3.
     Reiterates the basic facts of the break-in along with White House/CREEP tie-ins
with the persons employed. Author equates break-in, supposed governmental
security bugs, and treatment of Martha Mitchell to Mafia tactics. Speculates on
whether full investigation will be forthcoming.

10   July 24, 1972–**Time**, "Watergate Probe," p. 28.
     Justice Department investigating. Lawyer Douglas Caddy in jail on contempt
for refusing to disclose how he knew of arrest of burglars before any of them
called for legal representation. Money for bugging equipment traced to CREEP.

AUGUST 1972

11   August 14, 1972–**Newsweek**, "Watergate Trial," pp. 20-21.
     Recounts financial entanglements around $25,000 check from Kenneth
Dahlberg to Maurice Stans to Bernard Barker, $89,000 in Bernard Barker's
account from Manuel Ogarrio, phone calls between Bernard Barker and G. Gordon
Liddy. Republicans feel Watergate is a small ex-CIA/FBI adventurers' operation.

12   August 14, 1972–**Time**, "Watergate Contd.," pp. 21-22.
     Summary of Watergate events to date: arrests, Bernard Barker money,
E. Howard Hunt, G. Gordon Liddy, CREEP tie-in, plumbers, possible illegal
campaign donations.

13   August 19, 1972–**New Republic**, "Moral Novocain," p. 4.
     Post-Vietnam ethical apathy of public hit. Along with Watergate, milk and
ITT campaign payoffs, rush to get large donations before April 7 deadline
delineated.

14   August 28, 1972–**New York Times**.
     Investigation cannot be left up to the Administration–political ties too close.
President should appoint special independent prosecutor.

15   August 28, 1972–**Time**, "Watergate Issue," p. 20.
     While Democrats attempt to keep Watergate alive as an issue, more ties to
CREEP turn up: White House plumbers used E. Howard Hunt and G. Gordon
Liddy in the past and Bernard Barker payments eventually connect to Robert
Mardian.

16   August 29, 1972–**Washington Post**.
     President should make full disclosure of sources of campaign funds and
appoint special investigational and prosecutorial teams independent of government.

SEPTEMBER 1972

17 September 4, 1972–**Nation**, "Campaign '72," Carey McWilliams, p. 132.
Editorial deplores the possibility that Watergate facts may not be disclosed until after the election when they would have bearing on the outcome of the election.

18 September 4, 1972–**Newsweek**, "Skeleton in the GOP Closet," p. 38.
GAO charges Republicans with questionable bookkeeping. Examines where some funds came from and where they went.

19 September 4, 1972–**Time**, "Watergate Report," pp. 19-20.
Repeats GAO discoveries regarding $350,000 incorrectly received and disposed of, and recorded. Gerstein's Miami investigation also mentioned. Richard Kleindienst to investigate but close Republican ties should disqualify him.

20 September 9, 1972–**America**, "Watergate: The Republicans and the GAO," p. 138.
See *Time*, September 4, 1972.

21 September 11, 1972–**Time**, "Watergate Rolls On," pp. 18-19.
New developments: Democratic and Republican charges and countercharges of financial misdealings resulting from GAO investigation. Film of Democratic documents processed one week prior to Watergate for two burglars. Common Cause lawsuit filed.

22 September 15, 1972–**Life**, "But Will the Talk About the Watergate Never End?" pp. 32-33.
Summarizes post-Watergate events to date including firing or quitting of James McCord, G. Gordon Liddy, John Mitchell, and Hugh Sloan. The money from Bernard Barker's account is also traced to Maurice Stans and CREEP's Finance Committee. Five current investigations are mentioned along with Democratic lawsuit.

23 September 16, 1972–**America**, "Ready to be Served," Edward Glynn, p. 166.
See *Life*, September 15, 1972.

24 September 16, 1972–**Christian Science Monitor**.
Republicans should be anxious for speedy examination of Watergate and financial contributions to prove their claims of innocence.

25 September 18, 1972–**Nation**, "Public's Right to Know," pp. 195-96.
Both the financial irregularities and political espionage aspects of the case repeated. Selection of impartial investigator rather than Richard M. Nixon appointee Richard Kleindienst suggested.

26 September 18, 1972–**Newsweek**, "Spies Who Came in for the Heat," pp. 40-45.
Early revelation of origin, composition, actions of White House "plumbers,"

and their switch to anti-Democratic information-gathering given. Early attempts to burglarize Democratic National Convention, Bernard Barker money traced back through Mexican account to American sources, laundering of these funds and possible disclosure violations mentioned. Biographies of eleven major figures.

27 September 18, 1972—**Time**, "Watergate Taps," pp. 18-19.
Lawrence O'Brien charges his phones were tapped and conversations were monitored prior to Watergate and circulated as memo. Alleges Watergate Five tried to bug Capitol Hill Headquarters previously. Blames Richard Kleindienst for foot dragging. Democrats hire Walter Sheridan to investigate beyond seven indictees.

28 September 22, 1972—**Philadelphia Inquirer**.
Calls for impartial investigation.

29 September 23, 1972—**New Republic**, "Scandals as an Issue," pp. 8-9.
Watergate, questionable campaign funding seem not to affect voters except in growing cynicism. Republicans cutting themselves off from involvement has helped keep it from being a voter issue. Only if tie-in to higher-ups is made will this change.

30 September 25, 1972—**Nation**, "Zealots for Nixon: Gaudy Night at the Watergate," Robert Sherrill, pp. 230-34.
Satiric recap of Watergate events, likening actions and those involved with Adolph Hitler tactics. Backgrounds of key White House figures gone into in some detail, including Dwayne Andreas benefits from donations. FBI investigation expected to toe the Richard M. Nixon line.

31 September 25, 1972—**Newsweek**, "Dirty Business," Stewart Alsop, p. 126.
Watergate has had no impact to date on the campaign because: the ineptitude of the break-in itself lends comic overtones; too complex to delineate clearly for political purposes; little Democratic backing; people assume all politics is dirty anyway.

32 September 25, 1972—**Newsweek**, "Watergate: Now It's a Federal Case," pp. 31-32.
Lists Watergate indictments, both the Federal and in Florida. Case will rest on Alfred Baldwin testimony about casing Democratic National Convention offices and to whom he delivered tape transcripts. Trial may not begin until after the election.

33 September 25, 1972—**St. Louis Post-Dispatch**.
Nixon Administration has allowed doubt on integrity of law by halting civil suits until after elections and failing to appoint special prosecutor.

34 September 25, 1972—**Time**, "Seven Down on Watergate," p. 21.
With seven indicted, the Justice Department closes the case without further examining misuse of campaign funds. Possible Alfred Baldwin testimony mentioned. Wright Patman's committee ties Maurice Stans to Mexican laundering while he files countersuit to Lawrence O'Brien.

35 September 25, 1972—**U.S. News**, "What the 'Watergate Case' Is All About,"
    pp. 27-29.
Recapitulates information on origins of the caper, Republicans' and
Democrats' biographies, indictments, number and types of investigations underway, possible illegal campaign contributions, Democratic lawsuit, and Republican
countersuit.

36 September 25, 1972—**Washington Post**.
Until full disclosure is made, suspicion will increase about Republican
culpability.

37 September 29, 1972—**National Review**, "Watergate Hypothesis," p. 1054.
Why Watergate? Tells how the Administration felt the many press leaks
should be stopped, thus originating plumbers spying on staff to see who leaks and on
Democrats to see to whom information was leaked. Describes how the staff was
picked and handled so that higher-ups were shielded.

OCTOBER 1972

38 October 2, 1972—**Newsweek**, "Kennedy and Watergate," Stewart Alsop,
    p. 98.
Examines why Senator Edward Kennedy faces a difficult decision as to
whether his subcommittee should investigate Watergate. While accruing benefits
for the Democrats, he might find himself accused of political haymaking and/or
questioned regarding Chappaquiddick.

39 October 6, 1972—**Los Angeles Times**.
Deplores Judge John Sirica's prevention of further investigation due to
publicity and postponing of civil suits and congressional inquiry.

40 October 9, 1972—**Newsweek**, "Mitchell's Secret Fund," p. 39.
Reveals that John Mitchell dispensed secret funds for CREEP intelligence
for almost a year while he was Attorney General. Outlines large embursements to
G. Gordon Liddy, Jeb Magruder, Herbert Porter from Hugh Sloan with John
Mitchell's approval.

41 October 12, 1972—**New York Times**.
Deplores Republican instigated forging of Edmund Muskie letter. Reiterates
to voters that these are not common political practices but police state tactics.

42 October 23, 1972—**Nation**, "This Lawless Administration," Carey
    McWilliams, pp. 354-56.
Discusses attempts to stifle Alfred Baldwin confession-interview in *Los
Angeles Times*. Quotes Henry Fairlie in *Spectator* on "lawless" use of power to
gain and keep power—what it reflects on those involved and implications for lawless powerful presidency. Voters seem to feel better foreign business makes it
all right.

43 October 23, 1972—**Newsweek**, "Watergate: Very Offensive Security,"
    pp. 35-36.
    Reasons behind Watergate disruption of Democratic campaigns by "dirty tricks" explored—the "Canuck letter," bogus embarrassing phone calls, bogus mailings, computerized blackmail information. Donald Segretti tagged as the recruiter for the disruption network. His possible connection to Dwight Chapin in White House mentioned.

44 October 23, 1972—**Time**, "More Fumes from the Watergate Affair," p. 23.
    Links Donald Segretti to the White House: he was hired by Dwight Chapin and Gordon Strachan to subvert Democratic campaign, paid by Herbert Kalmbach. Several "dirty tricks" outlined, including forged Edmund Muskie letter. Senator Wright Patman's investigatory efforts fail, but Edward Kennedy takes up the gauntlet.

45 October 28, 1972—**New Republic**, "Corruption in the Campaign," pp. 5-7.
    Ties the moral corruption of Watergate with other campaign-related scandals—milk, ITT, grain sale to Russia. Examines potential shadiness of campaign donations and uses to which they were put. Ties CREEP spying to White House via Donald Segretti, Herbert Kalmbach, and Dwight Chapin.

46 October 28, 1972—**New Republic**, "Guilty Men," John Osborne, pp. 11-12.
    Recaps the Dwight Chapin-Donald Segretti-Herbert Kalmbach connections discussed on pages 5 through 7 of the same issue. Condensed press conference with Ronald Ziegler given, refusing to comment on these developments except to call them unsubstantiated. Clark MacGregor terms the stories politically oriented, while Richard M. Nixon indulges in typical press criticism.

47 October 30, 1972—**Newsweek**, "Dynamic Duo," pp. 76-77.
    Discusses how Carl Bernstein and Bob Woodward of *The Washington Post* first linked Watergate to White House aides. White House spokesmen attacks on press mentioned. In reply *Post* explains their duty to reveal the truth. No statements are made without being double checked.

48 October 30, 1972—**Newsweek**, "Story of a GOP Trickster," pp. 30-36.
    History of Donald Segretti's career, links to Dwight Chapin and H. R. Haldeman, hiring of Charles Svihlik as midwest disruptive agent explained. Outlines other Republican attempts to undermine American Party.

49 October 30, 1972—**Time**, "Denials and Still More Questions," pp. 18-19.
    Time now links Jeb Magruder to the break-in payments and the hiring of G. Gordon Liddy. Only one now-destroyed record of disbursements was kept. Allegations mentioned that Donald Segretti was coached in his grand jury statements. Reiteration of various White House spokesmen's condemnation of press criticism.

NOVEMBER 1972

50   November 6, 1972—**Time**, "How High?" p. 50.

Dwight Chapin admits to FBI involvement in setting up intelligence platoon and that Herbert Kalmbach paid Donald Segretti directly. Kalmbach admits to FBI he paid Segretti with CREEP money. No evidence to link H. R. Haldeman with the spying fund thus far.

51   November 10, 1972—**National Review**, "Watergate Idiocy," pp. 1231-32.

Editorial admitting that if Watergate is part of a planned group of activities, it is beyond the usual realm of political dirty tricks. If White House officers knew and approved, they lack professionalism and common sense, but public should not punish itself by electing McGovern.

52   November 11, 1972—**New Republic**, "After the Election," Eliot Marshall, pp. 11-12.

Likelihood of Watergate petering out examined. Trials and civil suits unlikely to bring out evidence linking it to White House because of limited scope of their coverage. Various pending civil suits described and why they are unlikely to have much result. Why Capitol Hill investigations are more likely to succeed.

BOOKS

53 **Perfectly Clear: Nixon from Whittier to Watergate**. By Frank Mankiewicz.
    New York Quadrangle/New York Times, 1973. 239p. $8.95.
    Written by Robert Kennedy's former press secretary and George McGovern's
national political campaign director. This book traces the political career of
Richard M. Nixon, showing how a lifelong history of dirty tricks culminated in
Watergate.
    The author begins with an examination of "dirty tricks" in others' cam-
paigns, Nixon practices in previous campaigns, the growth of intelligence operations
in and out of the country, listing of the "White House Horrors," biographies of
Watergate 5 and why the Cuban community responded to call to action, and
Watergate and the cover-up. Appendix contains Nixon on crime, list of criminal
statutes broken by Nixon, and McGovern on corruption. Indexed.

54 **Watergate and the White House: June 1972-July 1973**. Vol. 1. Ed. by
    Edward W. Knappman. New York, Facts on File, 1973. 246p. $4.25pa.
    Part I traces the evolution of Watergate from the break-in through John
Dean's testimony that the President had aided in the cover-up. Events, statements,
and court decisions are reported. Part II contains 250 editorials from 100 newspapers on various aspects of Watergate. A chronology of events is in the two inner
covers; brief biographies of those involved are provided. Indexed.

55 **Watergate: Chronology of a Crisis, Vol. 1**. Washington, D.C., Congressional
    Quarterly, 1973. 291p. $6.00.
    Arranged in chronological order, this book contains not only excerpts from
Congressional Quarterly (April-August 1973), but complete texts of many letters
and statements, as well as in-depth reportage of testimony at the Watergate hearings. Other articles cover: biographies, former White House scandals, indictments
and personnel changes, the hearings, proposed reforms, and hiring of the special
prosecutor. Index.

56 **Watergate Hearings: Break-In and Cover-Up**. By R. W. Apple. New York,
    Viking, 1973. 886p. $17.50. Bantam; $2.50pa.
    Edited by the *New York Times* staff, this book presents excerpted testimony
from the May-August 1973 hearings. To clarify the evidence, testimony is arranged
so as to point up their similarities and differences. An annotated chronology of
pertinent events from 1969 to 1973 is included, along with relevant presidential
statements and thumbnail biographies.

57 **Watergate: The Full Inside Story**. By Lewis Chester. New York, Ballantine,
    1973. 280p. $6.95.
    Compiled by four London *Times* staffers, this work covers events through the
Ervin hearings. There is some emphasis of the role of the press coverage and government attacks on it. Index.

JANUARY 1973

58 Vol. 38, 1973—**Albany Law Review**, "Thayer, Judicial Self-Restraint, and
    Watergate," Howard Sherain, pp. 52-65.
    In-depth examination of James Bradley Thayer's theory of judicial self-
restraint with summary of why this should not be applicable in possible Supreme
Court action on Watergate case.

59 Vol. 26/Number 1/1973—**Federal Communications Bar Journal**, "Electronic
    Eavesdropping, Wiretapping and Your Right to Privacy," Jeremiah
    Courtney, pp. 1-60.
    Examines how the Constitution, Congress, and F.C.C. through the years
have struggled with the dilemma of the expediency of electronic surveillance versus
the invasion of personal privacy. Claims national attention has been focused on the
continuing conflict by the Watergate caper and F.C.C. chairman's approval of the
monitoring of an employee's telephone.

60 January 15, 1973—**Newsweek**, "Watergate Opens," pp. 16-17.
    Opening Watergate trials seen as unlikely to try to trace the burglary to
White House. Repeats basic facts about the break-in and those involved.

61 January 16, 1973—**Newsday**.
    Deplores guilty pleas of four Watergate defendants because of possible deal,
thus stifling information. Cynical acceptance of Watergate as a political caper also
decried.

62 January 18, 1973—**New York Times**.
    Since criminal trials cannot expose string pullers, it is up to the Senate to
inquire. Guilty defendants may then testify without self-incrimination.

63 January 22, 1973—**Newsweek**, "Watergate: The Cast Shrinks," pp. 23-24.
    Potential case: Jeb Magruder and Herbert Porter requested intelligence infor-
mation from G. Gordon Liddy, who hired E. Howard Hunt, *et al.* Chances of
getting at truth diminish with Hunt guilty plea and possible following suit by
others. Thomas Gregory, a Brigham Young University student, testifies he was
hired by Hunt as an undercover agent to supply Democratic reports, floorplans
to CREEP.

64 January 22, 1973—**Time**, "Starting on Watergate," p. 19.
    See *Newsweek*, January 22, 1973.

65 January 29, 1973—**Nation**, "And Now There Are Two," pp. 131-32.
    With only two indictees left to plead, it may depend on the Ervin Committee
to elicit the truth of Watergate.

66 January 29, 1973—**Nation**, "Honors and Credits," pp. 132-33.
    Details the hiring of Brigham Young University student Thomas Gregory to
infiltrate Democratic campaigns and spy for Republicans for money and college
credits. BYU is now punishing him, but should they since presidential approval of
these activities was implied?

67   January 29, 1973—**Newsweek**, "Now It's the Watergate Two," pp. 24-25.
Four more defendants plead guilty. The fact of GOP hush money fund for defendants to avoid the embarrassment of a long trial is established. Alfred Baldwin testifies he turned tape transcripts over to a CREEP official he cannot remember.

68   January 29, 1973—**Time**, "Spy in the Cold," pp. 17-20.
Four defendants plead guilty at the behest of E. Howard Hunt, who promised them money while in jail. Remainder of article is an interview with Hunt on his philosophy and problems.

FEBRUARY 1973

69   February 1, 1973—**New York Times**.
Calls for intensive Senate inquiry.

70   February 2, 1973—**National Review**, "Meditations on Watergate," pp. 131-32.
Condones bugging and plumbing activities as necessary for national security. Realizes there are many questions which probably will not be answered within narrow trial definitions. Calls for complete disclosure from Republicans.

71   February 2, 1973—**Washington Post**.
Feels investigation important so public may draw lines as to legitimate campaign conduct, campaign funding, and government integrity.

72   February 3, 1973—**Christian Science Monitor**.
To restore public faith in judicial processes, Senate committee must investigate fully, in non-partisan and non-personal fashion.

73   February 3, 1973—**St. Louis Post-Dispatch**.
Calls for investigation by Senate.

74   February 5, 1973—**Newsweek**, "Rush to Judgment," p. 29.
Trial drawing to close. Judge Sirica questions lapse of memory of witness Alfred Baldwin. Hugh Sloan testifies he checked with John Mitchell and Maurice Stans about Jeb Magruder allowing large payments to G. Gordon Liddy. They OK'd but did not ask what the money was for.

75   February 12, 1973—**Nation**, "Angry Judges," pp. 196-97.
Judge Byrne in Ellsberg/Russo trial criticizes prosecution for delay in delivering material, indicates possible obstruction of justice. Judge Sirica deplores the limited examination of Watergate witnesses and failure to extend investigation in obvious directions.

76   February 12, 1973—**Newsweek**, "Watergate: Plenty to Probe," pp. 25-26.
Lists loose ends and unanswered questions at end of trial of Watergate Seven, including money laundering, possible limiting of case by government, and how high the knowledge of the operation went.

77 February 12, 1973—**Time**, "Verdict on Watergate," p. 11.
James McCord and G. Gordon Liddy convicted, but there has been no government attempt to see if responsibility goes higher. Only new evidence from Hugh Sloan. Liddy money OK'd by Jeb Magruder, Maurice Stans, and John Mitchell.

78 February 12, 1973—**U.S. News**, "Ahead: 'Phase Two' of Watergate Case," p. 88.
See *Time*, February 12, 1973.

79 February 17, 1973—**New Republic**, "Watergate Lies," Walter Pincus, pp. 11-14.
Through evasions and half-truths, CREEP sought to disassociate itself from Watergate burglars. This cover-up spelled out chronologically in detail.

80 February 19, 1973—**Newsweek**, "Watergate, Contd.," pp. 23-24.
Senate votes to launch its own investigation. Justice Department to investigate Donald Segretti's activities. Segretti's White House connections explored.

MARCH 1973

81 March 5, 1973—**Newsweek**, "Whispers About Colson," p. 21.
Increasing indications that Charles Colson sent E. Howard Hunt to investigate Edward Kennedy/Chappaquiddick and infiltrate Edmund Muskie's staff. Colson also set up White House "McGovern Watch" office to find, discuss, act on itineraries or any other information available. Also may have been involved in trying to quash Dita Beard's ITT flap.

82 March 12, 1973—**Time**, "Full Court Press," p. 20.
L. Patrick Gray confirmation hearings reveal the FBI links of E. Howard Hunt to Charles Colson and other presidential aids; the Mullen Company that E. Howard Hunt worked for at the time of the burglary is linked to CIA.

83 March 12, 1973—**Time**, "Subpeonas (Contd.)," p. 62.
Notes of reporters for *New York Times*, *Washington Post*, *Time*, and *Washington Star News* subpoenaed for Democratic and Republican lawsuits. These broadly stated subpoenas to be fought by the news agencies on the basis of privileged information.

84 March 14, 1973—**Los Angeles Times**.
By extending executive privileges, ordinarily used to protect policy-making efficiency, to cover former White House employees possibly criminally culpable, the President has harmed the concept of executive privilege and the Administration.

85 March 14, 1973—**New York Times**.
With his specious arguments for extending executive privilege to former White House employees, Richard M. Nixon would seem to be covering up possible White House involvement in Watergate.

86 March 14, 1973—**St. Louis Post-Dispatch.**
     Before acting on L. Patrick Gray's nomination as permanent FBI director, the Senate must hear John Dean and Dwight Chapin testimony, even if it means a head-on collision with the President over the concept of executive privilege.

87 March 19, 1973—**Newsweek,** "Watergate: A Sneak Preview," pp. 21-22.
     L. Patrick Gray's confirmation testimony links Donald Segretti to White House via Herbert Kalmbach payoffs at behest of Dwight Chapin. Also indicates CREEP gave false clues to FBI, sat in on interviews, and turned transcripts of others over to John Dean. Gray gave John Dean ITT memo.

88 March 19, 1973—**Time,** "Deepening Doubts About the Top Cop," pp. 13-14.
     See *Newsweek,* March 19, 1973.

89 March 20, 1973—**New York Times.**
     It is increasingly apparent that those close to the President, if not he himself, were involved in Watergate. Whether he is involved is moot, since he should accept responsibility and make full disclosure.

90 March 23, 1973—**Los Angeles Times.**
     By allowing himself to be used as a political tool, L. Patrick Gray has shown himself unqualified to be head of the FBI. It is up to Congress to be sure the new head has both independence and integrity.

91 March 24, 1973—**New Republic,** "Gray Clouds," pp. 7-8.
     L. Patrick Gray's appointment as FBI chief doubtful because of information he gave John Dean. Although Dean had recommended G. Gordon Liddy for his job, questions were raised about how the FBI and Gray could have been unaware of the connection. Gray also deliberately limited investigation to illegal bugging despite indications of other illegal activities: illegal campaign contributions and use of mails to defraud.

92 March 26, 1973—**Washington Post.**
     Deplores potential political showdown over blanket immunity. Suggests wisest course would be for Mr. Dean, *et al.*, to be allowed to testify voluntarily. If not, the issue should be stalwartly pursued.

APRIL 1973

93 April 2, 1973—**Newsweek,** "Growing Watergate Mess," pp. 14-18.
     James McCord to talk to Judge Sirica because of continued Sirica pressure and hope for lesser sentence. Speculates on what he might say. Nixon now shielding past and present staffers with executive privilege.

94 April 2, 1973—**Philadelphia Inquirer.**
     Quoting a 1952 Nixon speech, *Inquirer* feels he should follow his own advice and allow truth out. Although his men may testify before Federal Grand Jury, their findings are secret and under influence of the Justice Department. The only recourse is to full public disclosure by present and past White House staffers.

95 April 2, 1973—**Time,** "Crossfire Cuts Gray," pp. 12-13.
     Confirmation sure to be denied. Details on L. Patrick Gray's questionable handling of Watergate.

96   April 2, 1973—**Time**, "Man Everyone Wants to Hear From," pp. 12-13.
Discusses John Dean's influence on White House policy; biographical sketch of him.

97   April 2, 1973—**Time**, "Subpoenas (Contd.)," p. 65.
Outcome of subpoenas for Democratic lawsuit: quashed because such demands violate First Amendment.

98   April 2, 1973—**Time**, "Watergate's Widening Waves of Scandal," pp. 11-12.
See *Newsweek*, April 2, 1973.

99   April 4, 1973—**Los Angeles Times**.
White House staffers implicated in Watergate by secret James McCord testimony should be allowed rebuttal and refutation and not be shielded by Nixon-imposed conditions on their testimony.

100   April 4, 1973—**Newsday**.
Because John Dean's status as aide to the President with political responsibilities makes his testimony necessary, he should resign as in-house counsel, at least on Watergate. The President could then appoint a special outside counsel and Dean could testify. His continued silence will only increase suspicions.

101   April 4, 1973—**Washington Post**.
Denies Watergate outcry is an attempt to politically cripple the President. He crippled himself by not taking prompt action and allowing his men to testify.

102   April 7, 1973—**New Yorker**, "Notes and Comment," p. 31.
Had voters taken Watergate seriously before the election, they might have felt morally obligated to vote for McGovern against their better judgment. Now up to public whether to act or accept Watergate as norm of political behavior. Public cleansing seen as necessary to restore faith.

103   April 8, 1973—**New York Times**.
Although a link to H. R. Haldeman is possible, no evidence has been corroborated at this point, so Senator Weicker's call for his resignation incorrectly implies the entire committee's opinion. Such judgment must await appropriate testimony. President must relax executive privilege stand and stop muddying the waters.

104   April 9, 1973—**Chicago Tribune**.
L. Patrick Gray is the first casualty of Watergate fallout. If his actions were correct, the White House should have cleared him by making facts known. More people may be unfairly hurt, so all should cooperate to avoid further problems by complete disclosure.

105   April 13, 1973—**National Review**, "Watergate Flooding," pp. 406-407.
Alleges presidential misreading of how to handle Watergate has led to an unnecessary political fiasco. Continued silence points to cover-up and allows speculations to run rampant.

106 April 15, 1973—**St. Louis Post-Dispatch.**
The Watergate stench cannot be covered. The public is aware of it and becoming increasingly disenchanted with the political system.

107 April 16, 1973—**U.S. News**, "Watergate Case: What It's All About," pp. 27-29.
Repeats history of break-in, background of those involved, FBI and John Dean investigations, lawsuits, trial, L. Patrick Gray's Senate testimony, James McCord's secret testimony, and Richard M. Nixon's claim of executive privilege for present and former White House staff.

108 April 18, 1973—**Christian Century**, "Watergate and Secrecy," p. 444.
Calls for careful, unbiased handling of upcoming Ervin Committee hearings. Deplores fact that two men named for religious and American heroes are deeply involved—John Wesley Dean and Jeb Stuart Magruder.

109 April 19, 1973—**St. Louis Post-Dispatch.**
Richard M. Nixon's recent statement contains only two new facts—someone in the executive branch may be indicted, and he will permit aides to testify.

110 April 21, 1973—**New Republic**, "GOP Money Scandal," Walter Pincus, pp. 17-21.
In-depth examination of questionable campaign contributors, contributions, and Republican use of them and attempts to cover it up.

111 April 22, 1973—**New York Times.**
President's obstructionist tactics not as effective as in milk, wheat, ITT crises. President should choose new staff from trustworthy men of distinction rather than friends and enforce ethics from top down.

112 April 26, 1973—**Christian Science Monitor.**
To restore faith in the President, so he can become effective once again, full housecleaning and investigation by independent person necessary. Tendency to self-righteousness and imperiousness must also be curbed.

113 April 28, 1973—**New Republic**, "Fox Joins the Hounds," pp. 5-6.
With burgeoning scandals, Richard M. Nixon says he will now lead the pack to investigate; however, author cannot believe politically knowledgeable staff and President had no idea what tactics were employed. Original in-house investigator John Dean definitely involved.

114 April 29, 1973—**Washington Post.**
President should appoint special prosecutor, not try to "tough out" crisis as he has done with others with no attempt at change or amelioration. Weakened President cannot work effectively at home or abroad.

115 April 30, 1973—**Nation**, "In Character," pp. 546-47.
Lambasts Richard M. Nixon for being ten months late in his latest press conference and holding it only because of party pressures and imminent indictments. Encourages Democrats to push their lawsuit and insist on full disclosure.

116   April 30, 1973—**Newsweek**, "Long Trail of Denials to Credibility Gap,"
         p. 20.
Lists White House spokesmen's denials of White House involvement in Watergate from June 1972 through April 1973, then Ron Ziegler announces all these
previous statements "inoperative."

117   April 30, 1973—**Newsweek**, "Mr. Nixon's Super-Crisis," Stewart Alsop,
         p. 90.
Americans would prefer to think President not involved. To persuade people
of this, he now places himself in position of chief investigator. He will be hurt
primarily for his poor choice in employees.

118   April 30, 1973—**Newsweek**, "Watergate: The Dam Bursts," pp. 16-26.
Jeb Magruder's allegations that John Mitchell and John Dean knew in advance
of bugging, offered hush money and encouraged perjury has led to huge shake-up.
Richard M. Nixon now says he will lead new investigation while John Mitchell
admits he was queried in advance about Watergate but refused approval. Brief
biographical sketches of John Mitchell, John Dean, H. R. Haldeman, Jeb Magruder,
Charles Colson, Dwight Chapin, Gordon Strachan, Robert Mardian, Frederick
LaRue, Herbert Porter, Robert Odle, Sally Harmony, Herbert Kalmbach, and
Kenneth Parkinson.

119   April 30, 1973—**Time**, "Ripping Open an Incredible Scandal," pp. 11-17.
See *Newsweek*, April 30, 1973. Additional information: chronology of
events 3/23/73 through 4/14/73; Richard M. Nixon withdraws executive privilege;
Richard Kleindienst withdraws from investigation; John Dean to tell all; current
status of Democrat and Common Cause lawsuits given; "dirty tricks" against
Democratic candidates mentioned.

120   April 30, 1973—**Time**, "Sadness in Mid-America," Hugh Sidey, p. 18.
Author discusses impact of Richard M. Nixon cover-up on emotions in
Greenfield, Iowa. People object to underhanded methods for good ends. Nixon
blamed for Watergate rather than his underlings.

121   April 30, 1973—**U.S. News**, "Watergate: Was the President Deceived,"
         pp. 16-19.
Presents main points of Nixon's April 17 statement to the nation in which
he reported his own investigation of the Watergate had uncovered "major developments," and speculations about such developments by the press.

MAY 1973

122   May 1, 1973—**Chicago Tribune**.
Resignation of four top men in White House and Nixon speech points up
difference between United States and Britain, where such a situation could have
led to governmental collapse. Nixon was elected on the basis of his stands on issues,
and new administration would not necessarily be better.

123 May 1, 1973—**St. Louis Post-Dispatch.**
To protect against abuse inherent in system where government cannot be recalled, special independent prosecutor should be appointed.

124 May 2, 1973—**New York Times.**
While congressional moves to get special prosecutor are fine, it is ultimately up to the President to reinstitute candor, lawfulness, and constitutional practice, not by shuffling staff and claiming Watergate is a minor diversion from important business.

125 May 3, 1973—**Christian Science Monitor.**
Praises President for Richard Kleindienst and John Dean leaving as indication of clearing up Watergate and H. R. Haldeman and John Ehrlichman as toning down exaggerated executive authority. Hopes this will open better lines of communication between Congress and President.

126 May 3, 1973—**Wall Street Journal,** "Demand for a Special Prosecutor,"
        Arthur Schlesinger, Jr., p. 18.
Urges Nixon or Elliot Richardson to remove the investigation of White House involvement from the Department of Justice to an independent special prosecutor in order to clearly exonerate or implicate Nixon. Recommends impeachment should he be guilty of foreknowledge.

127 May 4, 1973—**Commonweal,** "Watergate," pp. 203-204.
Shows how Watergate has evolved from a mere building complex to a "caper," to a symbol of the ruthless hunt for power. Disputes Nixon contention of having no knowledge of or involvement in the cover-up.

128 May 5, 1973—**America,** "Duty of Citizen-Kings," p. 406.
Watergate has evolved from burglary to high administration cover-up in which even the President may be involved. Excessive public reaction could lead to loss of faith in system or refusal to view seriously because corruption inevitable. Our duty as citizens is to care for truth and justice.

129 May 5, 1973—**Business Week,** "Weakened White House: New Questions
        for Business," pp. 18-19.
Examines how the scandal and subsequent personnel shake-ups have left businessmen in confusion about who to deal with. Explains roles of H. R. Haldeman and John Ehrlichman with business, what Spiro Agnew's new duties may be.

130 May 5, 1973—**New Republic,** "There Can't be a Quick Fix," pp. 7-9.
Early preliminaries to Watergate lists three people with relevant information who could be called: Jack Bauman, Jack Stewart, Robert Fletcher. Several anti-Muskie dirty tricks should also be checked into, as well as the use of FBI to keep tabs on radical groups.

131 May 5, 1973—**New Yorker,** "Notes and Comment," pp. 33-34.
After ten months of apathy, sheer dint of truth is finally arousing public

opinion. Our system forces action on the truth, regardless of public opinion.

132   May 7, 1973—**Nation**, "Watergate: Phase IV," pp. 578-79.
Suggest this phase finds spotlight on President himself. Whether Nixon knew immaterial, because he is responsible, just as other "business managers" are for the illegal activities of their subordinates. Suggests naming irreproachable men as Attorney General, head of FBI, and special prosecutor as means of clearing the air.

133   May 7, 1973—**Newsweek**, "Government in Turmoil," pp. 22-34.
New developments: L. Patrick Gray burned E. Howard Hunt's files, resigns; Hunt and G. Gordon Liddy burgled Daniel Ellsberg's psychiatrist's office; John Ehrlichman and John Mitchell tied to Robert Vesco; more shady deals in return for campaign financing. Two contradicting stories of which White House aides did what outlined. Pressure increases to fire staff and hire special prosecutor.

134   May 7, 1973—**Newsweek**, "Poor Mr. Nixon," Stewart Alsop, p. 112.
After Bay of Pigs fiasco, J. F. Kennedy had 83 percent support, yet with no culpability proven, Nixon gets no sympathy. His own appointees and their attitudes, his own personality the cause. To recoup he must initiate major house-cleaning, end campaign corruption, prove he was not involved.

135   May 7, 1973—**Newsweek**, "Where Did All that Money Go?" pp. 24-25.
Outlines questionable campaign donors and promises given them: Robert Vesco and SEC troubles; Las Vegas gamblers, and Teamsters. Sources and disposi-tions of Maurice Stans, H. R. Haldeman, and Herbert Kalmbach funds and possible illegal uses of them given.

136   May 7, 1973—**Time**, "It Gets Worse: Nixon's Crisis of Confidence," pp. 16-18.
See *Newsweek*, May 7, 1973, "Government in Turmoil."

137   May 7, 1973—**Time**, "New Shocks—and More to Come," pp. 18-20.
L. Patrick Gray resigns and admits destroying papers from E. Howard Hunt's safe. Clamor increases for naming of special prosecutor and removal of Henry Petersen from the case. Describes tactics used to indicate false public support of Nixon policies.

138   May 7, 1973—**Time**, "Watergate Three," p. 82.
Story of how Barry Sussman, Carl Bernstein, and Bob Woodward of the *Washington Post* delved into and exposed the Watergate story.

139   May 7, 1973—**U.S. News**, "Watergate: Will Nixon Be the Big Loser?"
pp. 19-20.
Opinions of several congressmen and unnamed Administration aides regard-ing the effects of Watergate on Nixon's relations with Congress, foreign policy, the Republican party, and the presidency.

140   May 8, 1973—**Washington Post**.
      Suggests that, to avoid bias in selection of special prosecutor, Elliot Richardson leave selection to third party; prosecutor should be confirmed by Senate or Judiciary Committee, should be chosen immediately and be given broad authority.

141   May 9, 1973—**Wall Street Journal**.
      Decries tack of impeachment as a most serious and government-crippling step. It is unfair to condemn President with no solid facts.

142   May 11, 1973—**National Review**, "Unraveling," George F. Will, p. 514.
      Congratulates *Washington Post* for unearthing the scandals. Makes the point that those involved are not politicians.

143   May 12, 1973—**America**, "Watergate Comes Down," p. 434.
      President's April 30 speech a failure—did not clarify anything and confusion confounded by glowing terms describing two departing aides and coldness about the third (John Dean). Nixon fails to realize that the pattern of excessive power is the real problem.

144   May 12, 1973—**New Republic**. "President Buys Time," pp. 8-9.
      Questions President's supposed reactions to Watergate as described in his April 30 speech in relation to other facts. Suggests establishing investigatory committee under GAO auspices to check into campaign irregularities.

145   May 12, 1973—**New Republic**, "Something But the Truth," John Osborne, pp. 14-16.
      Speculates that atmosphere will not change with staff shifts because Nixon needs to be shielded by aides to function effectively. Alleges President lied in his speech and tells how and what he lied about.

146   May 12, 1973—**New Yorker**, "Notes and Comment," pp. 29-31.
      States bad presidents necessary to remind people what the office should be. Discusses how much presidential power should be delegated to others and who these others should be.

147   May 13, 1973—**New York Times Magazine**, "Constitutional Ervin," James M. McNaughton, p. 13+
      As chairman of Watergate Committee, Senator Sam Ervin is a symbol of Congress trying to regain its proper place. Discusses why Ervin was chosen, his contradictory views and how they are justified constitutionally. Examples of his anecdotal examination style.

148   May 14, 1973—**Nation**, "Grasp the Nettle," Robert Hatch, pp. 613-14.
      Encourages Congress to regain the power it is entitled to that has slipped to the presidency.

149   May 14, 1973—**Nation**, "Nixon Crowd," Robert Sherrill, pp. 611-13.
      Feels many of those around Nixon and involved in Watergate are ideological nuts who can justify any action on that basis. States Nixon could not have

been ignorant of his closest associates' actions. Repeats threads tying aides to Watergate. Cites 1972 campaign as typical in long line of Nixon sabotage campaigns.

150   May 14, 1973—**Nation,** "Too Little, Too Late," Carey McWilliams, pp. 610-11.
      Criticizes "housecleaning" and naming of new appointees as insufficient and dodging the issue. Finds Nixon's pleas of ignorance incredible. His latest speech raises more questions than it answered—examines them. Suggests special committee investigate the President's role in Watergate cover-up.

151   May 14, 1973—**Nation,** "Watergate Blotter," pp. 614-16.
      Chronologizes various statements of Nixon and his spokesmen regarding Watergate to show how these statements altered as time went by and new proof came out.

152   May 14, 1973—**New York Magazine,** "How the *Washington Post* Gave Nixon Hell," Aaron Latham, pp. 49-52+.
      Detailed account of how *Post* reporters Bob Woodward and Carl Bernstein uncovered momentous information linking the break-in with CREEP and the White House.

153   May 14, 1973—**Newsweek,** "Can Mr. Nixon Stay Afloat?" pp. 28-31.
      Delineates how Nixon is attempting to shore up Administration by staff shake-ups. Discusses damaging John Dean allegations and revelations of Daniel Ellsberg/John Russo trial. Paraphrases latest Nixon speech in which he announces departure of H. R. Haldeman, John Ehrlichman, and John Dean.

154   May 14, 1973—**Newsweek,** "Crazy Gang," Shana Alexander, p. 46.
      Only explanation of those involved in Watergate cover-up—insanity brought on by excessive power. Men of no moral weight who knew the law still failed to understand right and wrong.

155   May 14, 1973—**Newsweek,** "His Master's Voice," pp. 75-76.
      Reviews pre- and post-Watergate relations of the White House with the press. Examines Ron Ziegler's career and personality.

156   May 14, 1973—**Newsweek,** "How the World Looks at Watergate," pp. 49-50.
      Reviews international reactions to Watergate disclosures and what effects could be if the scandal widens further.

157   May 14, 1973—**Newsweek,** "John Dean Points a Finger," pp. 32-37.
      Complete Dean story from when he first head of break-in through his decision to talk. Others interviewed: Donald Nixon and Martha Mitchell. Donald Segretti indicted.

158   May 14, 1973—**Newsweek,** "War, Not Politics," Stewart Alsop, p. 132.
      States 1972 campaign unlike any other—resembled war, not politics. Compares dirty tricks, covert activities, to wartime occurrences.

159 May 14, 1973—**Time**, "Crowded Blotter of Watergate Suspects: A Checklist of Charges," pp. 19-20.
Lists areas in which 17 White House staffers are under investigation and their current employment statuses.

160 May 14, 1973—**Time**, "Good Uses of the Watergate Affair," Hedley Donovan, pp. 24-25.
Examines why Watergate brings some cause for rejoicing: unpopular "palace guard" eliminated, importance of free press proven, increased presidential power under check.

161 May 14, 1973—**Time**, "Guilty Until Proven Innocent," Hugh Sidey, p. 19.
Blames Watergate on isolation and secrecy of Nixon's Administration. Reflects doubts of other politicians as to his lack of involvement or knowledge.

162 May 14, 1973—**Time**, "Lawyers' Lawyers," pp. 69-70.
Professional backgrounds of the lawyers chosen by some of the prominent Watergate figures explored.

163 May 14, 1973—**Time**, "Nixon's Nightmare: Fighting to be Believed," pp. 17-32.
Recaps Nixon's latest Watergate speech, personnel changes, mood in the White House. New allegations: Daniel Ellsberg break-in White House engineered, offer of FBI directorship to Judge Byrne, White House taps. Traces White House intelligence efforts from 1969 on. Campaign "dirty tricks" also detailed. Process of impeachment briefly outlined.

164 May 14, 1973—**Time**, "Villain Vindicated," p. 100.
President Nixon praises role of investigatory press in Watergate coverage. Other indications of White House attempts at conciliating the press mentioned. Brief examination of how and why the press could make its disclosures about Watergate.

165 May 14, 1973—**U.S. News**, "Is Watergate Waterloo?" Howard Flieger, p. 116.
Discusses possible impact of Watergate on lame-duck presidency and upcoming elections.

166 May 14, 1973—**U.S. News**, "Nixon's Address to Nation on the Watergate Case," pp. 70-72.
Contains full text of Nixon's April 30th address.

167 May 14, 1973—**U.S. News**, "Watergate: As Nixon Picks Up the Pieces," pp. 17-19.
Enumerates the dismissals, resignations, and appointments which took place within Nixon's staff in his effort to rebuild the Administration after Watergate.

168   May 14, 1973—**U.S. News**, "Watergate: How the Lid Blew Off," pp. 20+
      Reviews events following the trial of the Watergate Seven which implicated "higher-ups" and led Nixon to begin his own investigation and restructure his staff.

169   May 15, 1973—**Vital Speeches**, "Watergate Affair," pp. 450-52.
      See *U.S. News*, May 14, "Nixon's Address to Nation on the Watergate Case."

170   May 16, 1973—**Christian Century**, "On Seeing the Presidency as Sacred," pp. 555-56.
      Suggests Nixon's April 30 address implies the presidency is a sacred office, the pursuit of which justifies dishonesty. Public seems to agree, because of their desire to absolve Nixon so "the office" won't be demeaned.

171   May 16, 1973—**Christian Century**, "Watergate and the Godfather Ethic," Martin E. Marty, p. 583.
      Author lists his reasons for *not* commenting on Watergate in his column. Relates Ronald Reagan's comment that guilty aides are not criminals because they felt they were acting rightly to the ethics of the Mafia, Manson, and Sirhan Sirhan.

172   May 17, 1973—**Wall Street Journal**, "Nightmare of Watergate," Irving Kristol, p. 20.
      A Nixon supporter sees the Watergate affair as a kind of madness and urges plausible explanations of their activities by those involved.

173   May 19, 1973—**Business Week**, "Ervin's Chief Investigator," p. 46.
      Profile of chief counsel Sam Dash—acknowledged expert in wiretapping, both legal and illegal. Government-funded Dash study not renewed because he denounced as unconstitutional John Mitchell's request of Supreme Court to allow non-court-ordered taps.

174   May 19, 1973—**New Yorker**, "Notes and Comment," pp. 27-28.
      Editorializes about how a few investigators toppled the well-oiled machine by showing how what once worked for its benefit contributed to its rapid breakdown under investigation.

175   May 20, 1973—**New York Times Magazine**, "Impeach the Speech, Not the President," William F. Buckley, p. 30+
      Criticizes the April 30th speech for lack of effectiveness and sense. Illustrates how close to monarchy the presidency has come. Imagines how Howard Hunt would have been recruited to Watergate team. Examines possible grounds for and ramifications of impeachment.

176   May 21, 1973—**Chicago Tribune**.
      Applauds choice of Archibald Cox as special prosecutor. Suggests if he finds evidence of presidential wrongdoing it be turned over to the House, he should grant immunity sparingly, and do job quickly.

177 May 21, 1973—**Nation**, "Press and Watergate," pp. 642-43.
Recent polls reflect failure of public to grasp the importance of Watergate.
It is not simply a political scandal, but a constitutional crisis. Cold War augmented
presidential power and furnished the technology, but this power has now been
delegated to faceless men. Lists corrections that must be made.

178 May 21, 1973—**Newsweek**, "And the Mess Goes On," pp. 16-21.
While latest speech and staff changes aim at bolstering Administration, new
developments—John Mitchell/Maurice Stans indictments in Robert Vesco case,
Daniel Ellsberg mistrial declared, and recent L. Patrick Gray and John Dean statements continue to undermine Nixon to the point that impeachment is increasingly
discussed.

179 May 21, 1973—**Newsweek**, "How Gray Tried to Warn Nixon," p. 18.
Details how L. Patrick Gray tried to inform Nixon that his aides were inter-
fering with the FBI investigation by making Watergate appear to be a CIA
operation.

180 May 21, 1973—**Newsweek**, "I Would Not Want the Presidency on Those
   Terms," Stewart Alsop, p. 108.
Deplores possibility of impeachment; compares present situation with that
of Andrew Johnson. Nixon will undoubtedly fight, but if forced into figurehead
status, might resign.

181 May 21, 1973—**Newsweek**, "Talk with John Dean," pp. 28-31.
Interview with Dean reveals he never gave Nixon a report on Watergate.
Claims attempts being made to cast him as scapegoat. While plea bargaining con-
tinues, he refuses to disclose all allegations.

182 May 21, 1973—**Time**, "Guide: Who's Investigating What," p. 15.
Brief biographies of Ervin Committee members, and other groups investigating Watergate.

183 May 21, 1973—**Time**, "Inquest Begins: Getting Closer to Nixon," pp. 16-28.
John Mitchell/Maurice Stans indicted in Robert Vesco case. Possible bomb-
shells to be dropped at Ervin hearings: Nixon aides interfered with FBI investigation; John Dean never gave Nixon report; James McCord urged to involve CIA;
Nixon held back information from Daniel Ellsberg trial. Lists witnesses to come
and possible testimony. Problems of television coverage explored.

184 May 21, 1973—**Time**, "Is Everybody Doing It?" pp. 32-33.
While polls show public believes Watergate to be typical political behavior,
this article shows few politicians or elected officials were involved, only Nixon
appointees.

185 May 21, 1973—**Time**, "Trying to Govern as the Fire Grows Hotter,"
   pp. 13-14.
Some current Watergate developments regarding involvement of CIA,
John Mitchell, and Maurice Stans. Biographies of new staff appointments made

to restore faith. How White House is attempting to change image and carry
on.

186   May 21, 1973—**U.S. News,** "Look at the Senate Committee Investigating
          Watergate," p. 18.
      List of committee members, delineation of their powers and rules, and
schedule of hearings.

187   May 21, 1973—**U.S. News,** "Now the Stage is Set for the Full Story,"
          pp. 17-19.
      Mentions who is investigating, indictments, Daniel Ellsberg break-in
connection, new Nixon staff appointments, and Senate criticism of press tactics.

188   May 21, 1973—**U.S. News,** "Stability of Our System Will Not Be Affected,"
          pp. 20-23.
      Interview with Alf Landon about past scandals, import of Watergate, and
how it may affect country.

189   May 21, 1973—**U.S. News,** "Watergate: Nixon's Mood at a Time of
          Trouble," pp. 24-25.
      Quotes unnamed sources reportedly close to Nixon who convey his outward
determination and private concern, and his characteristic strong reactions in times
of adversity.

190   May 21, 1973—**U.S. News,** "Watergate: Now the Stage Is Set for the Full
          Story," pp. 17-19.
      Recounts developments in the Watergate story prior to the opening of
the Ervin Committee hearings and reflects hope that these will lead to final
settlement of the case.

191   May 24, 1973—**St. Louis Post-Dispatch.**
      Deplores Nixon's establishment of a clandestine personal investigative task
force in 1970 for "national security" purposes, which mania for secrecy led to
Watergate. Suggests an unlimited press conference to help restore confidence.

192   May 24, 1973—**Wall Street Journal.**
      Calls for consensus of national feeling—presidential critics should speak only
on basis of fact and President should tell whole story to dispel growing
divisiveness in country.

193   May 25, 1973—**Commonweal,** "Scandal of a Political Philosophy," Peter
          Steinfels, pp. 279+
      Sees Watergate not just as a scandal but representative of the principles and
ethics of the Nixon Administration. Their philosophy was that the country had to
be protected from outspoken "mob" that had controlled it, by all-powerful
President using whatever means he felt were justified.

194   May 25, 1973—**National Review,** "Watergate: Shifting Perspectives,"
          pp. 565-66.

American and European public opinion on Watergate mild—only media and politicians in uproar. J. Edgar Hoover emerges as civil libertarian while aides seem more misguided than criminal. Nixon may become more liberal to appease opponents. Will Watergate swing balance in Congress against Nixon's programs? Foreign affairs position weakened.

195 May 26, 1973—**New Republic**, "Clandestine Corruption," pp. 5-6+
Shows how the financial link first led to exposure of CREEP involvement and how the CIA was used by the White House before and after Watergate. Also examines FBI laxity in investigation.

196 May 26, 1973—**New Republic**, "Speaking of Reform," p. 4.
Outlines faults in basic system that need altering: possibility of one party controlling presidency while other controls Congress; four-year presidential term with no recall option; one man rule. Defends use of TV for hearings. Criticizes John Mitchell as pseudo-law and order advocate.

197 May 26, 1973—**New Yorker**, "Notes and Comment," p. 33.
Watergate has led to the separation of two systems once thought to be "*the* system": constitutional system, and presidential system. Hopes members of rival institutions such as Congress, will now maintain their independence from the presidency.

198 May 27, 1973—**New York Times**.
Deplores police state tactics used by Administration to protect against our enemies in foreign police states. Security should be based on laws, elected officials, and citizens' goodwill.

199 May 28, 1973—**New Leader**, "Watergate Undertow," Andrew J. Glass,
pp. 5-6.
Presents aspects of the Watergate affair which qualify it as Nixon's "seventh crisis" and suggests possible political outcomes and casualties of the affair.

200 May 28, 1973—**Newsweek**, "Exposing the Big Cover-Up," pp. 26-31.
James McCord's testimony, further campaign money problems, John Mitchell scapegoat allegations all hurting Nixon. Archibald Cox to be named special prosecutor. James McCord testimony describes burglary, John Caulfield's hush attempts, and John Mitchell definitely involved. Brief biography of Caulfield. Robert Odle testimony reviewed. Herbert Kalmbach charged by GAO with using campaign funds for hush money.

201 May 28, 1973—**Newsweek**, "High Price of Security," pp. 33-40.
Examines attempts to use FBI and CIA to monitor "enemies," stop leaks—including Henry Kissinger's National Security Council, to cover-up or take the rap for Watergate.

202 May 28, 1973—**Newsweek**, "Mitchells Speak Up," pp. 30-31.
John and Martha Mitchell both allege someone is trying to make him a scape-goat—she says Nixon, he says no.

203   May 28, 1973—**Newsweek**, "Secret Agent Named 'Tony'," p. 38.
Traces hiring and investigations conducted by Tony Ulasewicz, political undercover agent, including Chappaquiddick on assignment from John Ehrlichman.

204   May 28, 1973—**Newsweek**, "Watergate on Camera," p. 113.
Discusses difficulties of presenting Watergate facts and developments on television as opposed to in print.

205   May 28, 1973—**Time**, "Defending Nixon," p. 61.
Various editors criticize other press members for harrassment of Nixon and rationalize his subordinates' actions.

206   May 28, 1973—**Time**, "How Main Street Views Watergate," pp. 13-19.
Interviews with people in five communities regarding Watergate.

207   May 28, 1973—**Time**, "Newest Daytime Drama," pp. 20-24.
Background of James McCord decision to talk. Chronology of current occurrences according to McCord. John Caulfield's contradictory testimony presented; style of various committee members mentioned. Robert Odle's testimony repeated.

208   May 28, 1973—**U.S. News**, "On the Record: Claims of White House 'Payoff'," pp. 22-28.
See *Time*, May 28, "Newest Daytime Drama."

209   May 28, 1973—**U.S. News**, "Watergate Upheaval: Can Nixon Still Govern? Answers from Across U.S.," pp. 20-21.
Summarizes general sentiments expressed in an informal nationwide survey of business and government people regarding the influence of Watergate on Nixon's leadership effectiveness.

210   May 28, 1973—**U.S. News**, "Watergate Upheaval: Is Government at a Standstill?" pp. 17-19.
A run-down on the numerous shifts and vacancies in Administration posts since Watergate and statements as to their effect on government functioning by identified and anonymous persons.

211   May 28, 1973—**U.S. News**, "Why the Senate Is Investigating Watergate," Sam J. Ervin, Jr., pp. 106-107.
Full text of opening remarks by Chairman Sam Ervin as the Senate Select Committee on Presidential Campaign Activities began its hearing on May 17, 1973.

212   May 30, 1973—**Christian Century**, "Watergate: 'Just Politics'?" Reese Cleghorn, pp. 620-21.
Deplores the real possibility that public may dismiss Watergate corruption as "just politics." Recaps recent poll in *Charlotte Observer* (N.C.) which supports this view. Expresses hope that more familiarity with the circumstances will change public apathy.

JUNE 1973

213   June 1973—**Ebony**, "With Thanks to Frank Wills," pp. 94-95.
Outlines what Watergate security guard Frank Wills did to blow the whistle on the buggers and what it led to.

214   June 1973—**Fortune**, "While We're Waiting for the Verdict," p. 111.
Shows what programs are in abeyance while Watergate occupies President and country. Advocates personnel changes, increasing importance of Congress and Cabinet to restore public's faith.

215   June 1973—**Harvard Journal of Legislation**, "Executive Privilege and the Congressional Right of Inquiry," Robert C. Randolph and Daniel C. Smith, pp. 621-71.
Discusses the problem of executive control of congressional sources of information and examines executive privilege doctrine and political sanctions available to Congress. Points out developments during Nixon Administration which indicate increasing control of information by the Executive.

216   June 2, 1973—**Business Week**, "Watergate: Nixon's Angels Stand Firm," pp. 21-22.
Nixon backers still committed to him, but favor tougher contribution laws. Their suggestions for changing the laws repeated.

217   June 2, 1973—**New Republic**, "Ervin Hearings," pp. 7-8.
James McCord tells of attempt to tie Watergate to CIA and buy his silence. John Caulfield corroborates clemency attempt. Gerald Alch denies he proposed CIA defense or knew of clemency. Describes Democratic senators on committee as low-color and not well prepared. Assesses capabilities of others on committee. Their investigation will include political sabotage and funding.

218   June 2, 1973—**New Republic**, "Limited Confession," John Osborne, pp. 14-15.
Discusses seven statements in Nixon's May 22nd "confession." Feels they were made to protect himself from future testimony of employees: confessed to starting domestic surveillance procedures in 1969, some illegal, and used in 1972. Also restricted investigation of Watergate for national security, but no cover-up involvement.

219   June 2, 1973—**New Republic**, "Puzzling Prosecution," Walter Pincus, pp. 15-19.
Earl Silbert and Henry Petersen either owed Justice Department job to, or worked with, John Mitchell and John Dean. These prosecutors' efforts to be scrutinized. Their investigation limited to wiretap only—other possible violations not pursued and trial unnecessarily slow. Details questionable FBI activities and policies.

220   June 2, 1973—**New Yorker,** "Notes and Comment," pp. 25-26.
Satirically compares actual facts with presidential facts. Shows how once impervious presidential facts now melt away. Queries whether Nixon's failure to read newspapers put him at a disadvantage.

221   June 4, 1973—**Nation,** "Case for Resignation," pp. 706-707.
Now that President has accepted responsibility for the cover-up, what should be done? Discusses pros and cons of impeachment and resignation.

222   June 4, 1973—**Nation,** "Watergate: A Brush with Tyranny," Ramsey Clark, pp. 712-14.
Asserts that a value system undermines law, which should be applied disinterestedly and not on a value basis. Examines how politicians appointed to Justice Department used political rather than legal judgments.

223   June 4, 1973—**Newsweek,** "Back to Live Drama," Cyclops, p. 59.
Reviews the television hearings, comparing them with earlier Kefauver, Army-McCarthy ones. Talks of impact on viewer, Senators emerging as heroes.

224   June 4, 1973—**Newsweek,** "Hearings Under Cover," pp. 26-28.
James McCord's second week of testimony, also John Caulfield on hush attempts; Tony Ulasewicz; Gerald Alch; Bernard Barker; and Alfred Baldwin.

225   June 4, 1973—**Newsweek,** "Mr. Nixon States His Case," pp. 16-26.
Covers Nixon's semi-confession of men around him involved in cover-up, his own sanction of secret operations. Compounding accusations, indictments, and their effect on government explained. Nixon justifies on basis of national security. Claims he limited Watergate investigation because feared CIA link.

226   June 4, 1973—**Newsweek,** "Spreading Stain: Justice . . . FBI . . . CIA . . . State . . . SEC," p. 25.
Extent to which each of these agencies has been smeared by Watergate, including shady dealings, staffers compromised.

227   June 4, 1973—**Time,** "John Dean Warns: A Mile to Go," pp. 30-31.
Interview with John Dean about why he is testifying, reaction to recent Nixon statements, pre-plumbers White House mood.

228   June 4, 1973—**Time,** "Nixon's Thin Defense: The Need for Secrecy," pp. 17-23.
Nixon defends plumbers and cover-up on basis of national security. How his 4,000 word legal statement was written. Parts of his statement excerpted and commented on.

229   June 4, 1973—**Time,** "Tales from the Men Who Took Orders," pp. 26-30.
John Caulfield, James McCord, Tony Ulasewicz, Gerald Alch, Bernard Barker, and Alfred Baldwin testimony. Hugh Sloan's potential testimony outlined.

230   June 4, 1973—**U.S. News**, "Nixon Tells His Side of the Watergate Case,"
      pp. 96-99.
      Complete text of Nixon's May 22nd statement on Watergate.

231   June 4, 1973—**U.S. News**, "President Fights Back," p. 15.
      Summarizes Nixon's May 22nd speech denying complicity in the Watergate
break-in, press reception to the speech and current events involving the President.

232   June 4, 1973—**U.S. News**, "Watergate and the CIA," p. 19.
      Gives a run-down on the allegations included in testimony before Senate
committees linking Watergate, the CIA, and the White House.

233   June 4, 1973—**U.S. News**, "Where Watergate Stands Now," pp. 16-18.
      An update on the first two weeks of Sam Ervin committee hearings, point-
ing out conflicts in testimony and answers to what the article calls "key questions"
in the investigation.

234   June 6, 1973—**Christian Century**, "Whispered in Private Rooms . . . Shouted
      from the Housetops," Robert Jewett, pp. 648-50.
      Long history of overzealous nationalism led to nonchalant Watergate
illegalities. National self-respect can only come when the law is carried out, showing truth to be more important than any elected official.

235   June 8, 1973—**National Review**, "As It Might Have Gone," William F.
      Buckley, Jr., p. 650.
      Mythical speech Nixon should have delivered admitting blame of those close
to him and of himself for being so isolated it could happen.

236   June 8, 1973—**National Review**, "PEPCO Implicated," Joseph C. Goulden,
      p. 619.
      Satirical article about how the company supplying electricity to E. Howard
Hunt's office could have been subject to White House influence and tracing that
influence to ridiculous lengths.

237   June 8, 1973—**National Review**, "President Agnew," pp. 615-18.
      As investigation widens, Nixon becomes more imperiled. Nixon supporter
Barry Goldwater used as index to change in party confidence. Contemplates how
an Agnew Administration would differ from Nixon's.

238   June 8, 1973—**St. Louis Post-Dispatch**.
      Feels Cox is wrong in wanting to put limits on John Dean and Jeb
Magruder immunity and eliminate television-radio coverage.

239   June 9, 1973—**New Republic**, "All Deliberate Speed," pp. 7-8.
      Unhurried fashion of hearings has allowed Alfred Baldwin to testify that he
made carbons of all transcripts, a fact heretofore not mentioned or investigated.

240   June 9, 1973—**New Republic**, "Subpoenaing the President," Nathan Lewin,
      pp. 19-21.

One of the many recent grand jury leaks regarding possible subpoenaing of the President discussed. Various precedental Supreme Court decisions examined. The possibility and legal aspects of indicting a president also examined.

241 June 9, 1973—New Republic, "Watergate vs. the Soaps," Sedulus, pp. 23-24.
Like Bernard Barker, the public seems to prefer not to know what happened but prefer soaps. Many phoned objecting to pre-empting. Watergate star is an off-camera President so not as dramatic as the Kefauver or McCarthy hearings.

242 June 9, 1973—New Yorker, "Letter from Washington," Richard H. Rovere, pp. 103-109.
Discusses why foreign governments have not taken advantage of Nixon's diminished power due to Watergate. Examines pros and cons of impeachment. Compares present Cabinet with past one. One sure result of Watergate will be diminution in the power of the presidency.

243 June 9, 1973—New Yorker, "Notes and Comment," p. 25.
Discusses Republican "game plan" for their convention, which involved using supposed radicals in supposed opposition, to enlist sympathies of middle America. Other dirty tricks mentioned including phony mailings and polls.

244 June 9, 1973—New Yorker, "U.S. Journal: The Midwest," Calvin Trillin, pp. 84-87.
Anecdotal article on how the Midwest, particularly Kansas, reacts differently from the East or West coasts on Watergate.

245 June 10, 1973—New York Times Magazine, "Inflation, Frustration and Tea," J. H. Plumb, pp. 20+
English intellectuals wonder why Watergate has not led to outcry for constitutional reform, making President more readily accountable. The rest of the British public pays little attention to the scandal now, though.

246 June 11, 1973—Nation, "Why They Did What They Did," pp. 738-40.
Delineates political motivations which led to formation of plumbers and Watergate, and the subsequent cover-up.

247 June 11, 1973—Newsweek, "Cox Team: On the Case," p. 22.
Cox removes three attorneys who worked on Watergate in the past. Sketches of a few members of the new prosecution team.

248 June 11, 1973—Newsweek, "Nixon into Nixxon," Shana Alexander, p. 35.
Watergate, like "The Blob," continues to grow and change and only fresh air of televised hearings can end it. Chief actors also metamorphosize: Daniel Ellsberg, James McCord, Ronald Ziegler, Henry Kissinger, and Richard Nixon.

249 June 11, 1973—Newsweek, "Watergate: The Eye of the Storm," pp. 19-24.
Some of John Dean's potential charges listed. Substance of Haldeman/ Ehrlichman testimony before Senate subcommittee on intelligence operations regarding interference with FBI investigation and attempts to involve CIA repeated.

Further leaks bring up more questions about presidential homes, contributions, friends. White House planned to plant "friend" on committee but unsuccessful.

250   June 11, 1973—**Newsweek**, "What the Secret Police Did," pp. 20-1.
    Rundown of plumbers plans and activities under investigation. Robert Mardian thought to be closely involved. His testimony in brief.

251   June 11, 1973—**Time**, "Immunity Game," p. 96.
    Brief history of immunity and past cases of it, why and how used. John Dean can only be offered "use" immunity under new law. Dean does not want to plead guilty to obstruction of justice because of disbarment. Further prosecution would be difficult since his testimony could not be used.

252   June 11, 1973—**Time**, "Of Memory and National Security," pp. 19-21.
    In testimony before Senate appropriations subcommittee, H. R. Haldeman and John Ehrlichman deny trying to involve CIA in Watergate or claim to have forgotten. If it was done, it was for national security. Possibility of subpoenaing President quashed by Ronald Ziegler statement.

253   June 11, 1973—**U.S. News**, "Spying at White House Orders," pp. 19-21.
    Lists internal intelligence attempts of the Administration, why they were initiated, how they led to plumbers, and national security reasons cited by the Administration.

254   June 13, 1973—**Chicago Tribune**.
    Calls for continuation of public hearings—no prejudicial publicity so far except from secret testimony, but cautions senators to question judiciously and fairly.

255   June 13, 1973—**New York Times**.
    Does not feel limited immunity for John Dean wrong since his testimony will be beneficial but will not prejudice other legal actions against him.

256   June 14, 1973—**Christian Science Monitor**.
    Commends Judge John Sirica's decision to allow television coverage of Watergate hearings. It need not interfere with future prosecutions and public should be informed.

257   June 14, 1973—**Wall Street Journal**.
    Some hoped-for reforms may come out of this—full campaign fund disclosure, less public tolerance of Administration secrecy, clearer delineation of powers of investigatory agencies.

258   June 14, 1973—**Wall Street Journal**, "What Comes Next, after Watergate?"
        Irving Kristol, p. 16.
    Rejects the possibility of impeachment and discusses damage done by Watergate to neo-conservatism and business-in-politics.

259   June 16, 1973—**America**, "Quite a Difference," Mary McGrory, p. 550.
      Charts the difference between the Watergate hearings and the Army-McCarthy
hearings.

260   June 16, 1973—**New Republic**, "How the FBI and CIA Played the Game,"
         Walter Pincus, pp. 19-23.
      Why the White House wanted the investigation stopped. In-depth chronology
of early cover-up, FBI activities, and attempts to involve CIA.

261   June 16, 1973—**New Republic**, "Prosecution and Publicity," pp. 5-6.
      Detailed discussion why Watergate should be televised in opposition to Archi-
bald Cox request: because this is too complex and more than just a criminal case.

262   June 18, 1973—**Nation**, "Supremacy and Secrecy: The Deeper Meaning of
         Watergate," Wayne L. Morse, pp. 777-79.
      Warns against tendency toward executive supremacy and police state. Replies
to Nixon's statement involving national security as reason for plumbers and aborted
intelligence unit.

263   June 18, 1973—**Newsweek**, "John Dean: The Secret-Sharer," p. 20.
      Biography of John Dean and his role in Watergate.

264   June 18, 1973—**Newsweek**, "Path from Loyalty to Perjury," pp. 28-39.
      Testimony of Herbert Porter, Sally Harmony, Hugh Sloan, and Robert Reisner.
Hearings to continue on television despite Archibald Cox objections about prejudice
to future trials.

265   June 18, 1973—**Newsweek**, "Seventh Crisis Heats Up," pp. 19-24.
      Much of government at standstill under attack. John Dean's allegations:
Nixon knew of cover-up, milk contributions; White House pressured judge in Watergate civil suit; Charles Colson suggested bombing Brookings Institute; FBI list of
past presidential abuses of it; consideration of assassination of Panama's president;
taxes used to pressure George Wallace. H. R. Haldeman and John Ehrlichman depo-
sitions given.

266   June 18, 1973—**Time**, "Crossfire on Four Fronts," pp. 14-20.
      Covers the week's testimony. Sally Harmony admits typing and destroying
tape transcripts. All aides Hugh Sloan consulted about his testimony suggested perjury or Fifth Amendment. John Ehrlichman ties John Mitchell to directly ordering
break-ins. Hoover disapproved secret intelligence unit. Attempt to drag in CIA
mentioned.

267   June 18, 1973—**Time**, "President Shores Up His Command," pp. 11-14.
      Explains new appointments, Nixon activities to shore up command. Recently
published CIA memos undercut Nixon's May 22 contentions that Watergate was
created out of national security. John Dean, Charles Colson and Herbert Kalmbach
statements hinted at. Cox's attempts to block televising the hearings stated.

268   June 18, 1973—**Time**, "Watergate Issues, 1: Is Publicity Dangerous?" pp. 61-2.
    Hearings scored by *London Times* for promoting hearsay evidence, no cross
examination. Publicity can only complicate future prosecutions. Presents various
legal opinions on the subject of pretrial publicity.

269   June 18, 1973—**Time**, "Watergate Issues, 2: Must a President Testify?" p. 62.
    Discusses precedents and opinions on subpoenaing the President.

270   June 18, 1973—**U.S. News**, "Day after Day, More Revelations about Water-
        gate," pp. 20-1.
    Repeats H. R. Haldeman and John Ehrlichman depositions in Democratic law-
suit. Herbert Porter, Hugh Sloan, and Sally Harmony testimony also given.

271   June 18, 1973—**U.S. News**, "How Washington's Scandal Will Affect U.S.
        Politics," pp. 22-4.
    Possible impact of Watergate on future Republican and Democratic campaigns
analyzed by U.S. governors—feel not too much impact for Democrats in state and
local campaigns. Some possible future presidential candidates evaluated.

272   June 18, 1973—**U.S. News**, "Watergate—Where Will It All Lead?" pp. 17-19.
    Discusses potential problems inherent with President under fire. Archibald
Cox asked Ervin Committee to delay televised hearings so as not to prejudice
trials necessary to restore faith in institutions, then filed suit but it failed. Some
opinions pro and con of people around the country.

273   June 18, 1973—**U.S. News**, "Why Senator Ervin Presses Ahead," p. 19.
    Interview asks Sam Ervin why he goes on instead of heeding Cox's request.
He feels if he acquiesced, postponement would be continuous and publicity
increase. Mail supports this stance.

274   June 21, 1973—**Washington Post**.
    Calls for clear-eyed appraisal of upcoming, potentially explosive John Dean
testimony.

275   June 22, 1973—**National Review**, "Deeper and Deeper," pp. 666-67.
    Lists contentions of General Vernon Walters' memos on conversation with
John Ehrlichman, H. R. Haldeman, John Dean, and L. Patrick Gray regarding
attempts to involve CIA in cover-up. Critizes the leaks by John Dean, the hearings,
and Archibald Cox.

276   June 22, 1973—**National Review**, "Immunity for Everyone?" p. 703.
    Questions the validity of plea bargaining in Watergate, since underlings may
be tempted to gain immunity by inflating the case against their superiors.

277   June 23, 1973—**New Republic**, "Honorable Men, All," pp. 6-7.
    Committee did not fare well in questioning Maurice Stans. They failed to pin
him down on sources of information, why he did or did not do certain things,
where money came from or went to and why he didn't question large cash outlays.

278   June 23, 1973—**New Yorker**, "Notes and Comment," pp. 25-6.
Discusses Nixon's attempt to establish a central intelligence network based in the White House in 1969 and how this disbanded plan sowed seeds for plumbers and Watergate. Decides the only time Nixon worked positively for the country was as Vice President.

279   June 25, 1973—**Newsweek**, "Colson Connection," pp. 24-5.
Thus far Charles Colson involvement vague and unprovable—claims he never knew what was going on. Biographical information on his background.

280   June 25, 1973—**Newsweek**, "Day That Will Live in Infamy," pp. 20-1.
One year later, reactions to Watergate. They vary from humor-buttons and bumper stickers, to proliferation of books, to rampant fear of bugging.

281   June 25, 1973—**Newsweek**, "Inside Watergate," pp. 19-24.
Covers Jeb Magruder's testimony detailing planning, approval, financing and cover-up of Watergate and Maurice Stans testimony claiming ignorance. Memo showing John Ehrlichman approval of Daniel Ellsberg break-in turns up.

282   June 25, 1973—**Newsweek**, "Watergate and the Liberals," Stewart Alsop, p. 96.
Objects to massive Justice Department leaks—although they led to Watergate unfolding. Traditional legal safeguards (secret grand jury) flouted and no one minds.

283   June 25, 1973—**Time**, "Critique from London," p. 96.
American press answers critical *London Times* editorial about press and television treatment of Nixon as "lynch law."

284   June 25, 1973—**Time**, "High Noon at the Hearings," pp. 9-14.
Lists probable contents of John Dean testimony. Covers Jeb Magruder's testimony: who he implicates and origins of Watergate and cover-up. Also Maurice Stans testimony regarding funding and his ignorance of destination of monies.

285   June 25, 1973—**Time**, "Watergate on TV: Show Biz and Anguished Ritual," Stefan Kanfer, pp. 14-15.
While television may present problems, in this case, it has reduced people and events involved to ordinariness, made it accessible and interesting. Views Senators as their roles and personalities have evolved. Television provides the stage for our modern classic tragedy.

286   June 25, 1973—**Time**, "Watergate Wit," p. 94.
Covers comedy acts, radio-television shows, record albums, and bumper stickers about Watergate.

287   June 25, 1973—**U.S. News**, "Agnew: Senate Hearings 'Can Hardly Fail to Muddy the Waters of Justice'," p. 26.
Criticizes effects of Committee for these reasons: no cross-examination, counsel use abridged, no assured rebuttal of witnesses; allows hearsay, inferences, impressions; allows cameras, which could be prejudicial.

288   June 25, 1973—**U.S. News**, "Due Process—A British View," p. 92.
    Excerpts from *London Times* editorial critical of newspaper handling of Nixon
and Watergate in prejudicial style.

289   June 25, 1973—**U.S. News**, "Problems in Trying to Damp Down Watergate,"
        pp. 24-6.
    Jeb Magruder and Maurice Stans testimony. Cox attempts to halt televised
hearings to no avail.

290   June 27, 1973—**Christian Century**, "'. . . And Nathan Said to David': A Water-
        gate Parable," J. Claude Evans, pp. 705-706.
    Draws parallels between story of David and Bathsheba and Watergate sins.
Criticizes Billy Graham for not undertaking role of Nathan and confronting Nixon
with his sins. Press deserves praise; balance of power to be reinstated.

291   June 28, 1973—**Los Angeles Times**.
    Repelled at idea of using IRS to "get" White House enemies. Calls for thor-
ough investigation of IRS.

292   June 28, 1973—**Wall Street Journal**.
    Administration attacks on John Dean will not rebut his testimony. Best
approach is for President to come up with all available material to challenge John
Dean.

293   June 29, 1973—**Chicago Tribune**.
    Contends list of White House enemies irrelevant to Watergate and similar
things should not turn hearings into free-for-all that would impair future trials.

294   June 30, 1973—**Christian Science Monitor**.
    Watergate cannot be justified on basis that "everyone does it," because they
do not. Elected officials must not simply obey the law, they must *uphold* it, which
Nixon seems not to have done.

295   June 30, 1973—**New Republic**, "Latest Cover-Up," Walter Pincus, pp. 14-17.
    Examines three stages of Watergate cover-up and how they fell apart plus
White House reaction to each stage.

JULY 1973

296   July 1973—**Current**, "Role of the Presidency, pp. 3-26.
    Symposium features Robert Brustein on Watergate as Greek tragedy (Richard
Nixon as Oedipus), *New Yorker*, May 26, 1973 editorial, Henry Steele Commager
on Watergate as catharsis, *Irving Kristol article from *Wall Street Journal*, May 17,
1973, Arthur Schlesinger on how to save the presidency, Theodore Hesburgh on
moral malaise of Watergate, John Gardner on how to overcome Watergate, Robert
Bowie on Watergate and foreign policy, and an editorial from *Nation*, June 4,
1973.

297 July 1973–**Current**, "What Must Be Done," John W. Gardner, pp. 19-21.
Advocates telling whole Watergate story; restoration of Congress as an equal branch of government; Congress should institute reforms; and Administration should reopen channels of communication.

298 July 1973–**Fortune**, "Getting at the Roots of Watergate," A. James Reichley, pp. 90-3+
Some roots in political corruption–examples of prominent politicians convicted or indicted. Current Washington standards condone questionable practices. Another root government emphasis and increased technology of intelligence gathering. Also excessive money and accent on President over other branches. Reforms needed: campaign financing, better legal means of handling dissent and leaks, more responsive presidency.

299 July 1973–**Society**, "Watergate: On Campaigns and Government Anarchy," T. L. Becker, pp. 12-13.
Satiric discussion of Richard Nixon campaign tactics and "punishments to fit the crime."

300 July 1, 1973–**New York Times Magazine**, "Is America Burning?" James Michener, pp. 10-11+
Personal reactions of author Michener who, although a Democrat, worked with some of those involved in Watergate. Examines results of other national traumas to see what this latest might bring. Discusses possible outcomes for Richard Nixon and benefits for the country.

301 July 2, 1973–**Nation**, "Cover-Up of the Cover-Up," pp. 2-3.
Shows how complexity of cover-up had to dissolve and what attempts were made to cover the cover-up. This entails all disclaiming of presidential involvement down to last line of Haldeman/Ehrlichman. Clamor grows for full disclosure by Richard Nixon.

302 July 2, 1973–**New Yorker**, "Notes and Comment," pp. 21-3.
Explains why partisanship in the Senate inquiry is unlikely, although some are trying to promote it, and why it could be so damaging.

303 July 2, 1973–**Newsweek**, "From the Summit to the Moment of Truth," pp. 13-16.
Possible John Dean testimony explored, including Liddy discussion of burglary in front of Mitchell; cover-up; use of tax audits; attempts to "fix" committee and influence Senator Howard Baker. Administration efforts to discredit Dean outlined.

304 July 2, 1973–**Newsweek**, "Money Game," pp. 16-17.
More campaign fund uses come to light: use for hush money, eliciting funds from people with government problems, some unaccounted-for funds used for personal things.

305 July 2, 1973–**Time**, "Guerilla Warfare at Credibility Gap," pp. 12-16.
See *Newsweek*, July 2 "From the Summit to the Moment of Truth."

306 July 2, 1973–**Time**, "White House Intrigue: Colson vs. Dean," p. 14.
Possible Charles Colson ties to Watergate. Evidence of John Dean's obstruction of justice. Colson's explanation of his actions.

307 July 2, 1973–**U.S. News**, "Watergate Moves into a Crucial Stage," pp. 25-6.
Anticipates John Dean's testimony before the Ervin committee and recaps testimonies given by others, through June 22, which implicates or clears Richard Nixon of involvement in Watergate break-in and cover-up.

308 July 4, 1973–**Christian Century**, "Ethics Student Rationalizes Watergate," pp. 723-4.
Disproves Jeb Magruder's allegation that his illegal activities rationalized by former ethics teacher William Sloan Coffin's illegal anti-war activities. One is a secret, and one is a public challenge of possible constitutional violations. Watergate challenges us to hold elected officials firm to higher ethical authority.

309 July 6, 1973–**National Review**, "Sauerkraut Ice Cream," George F. Will, p. 726.
Compares Richard Nixon and White House, later self-contradicted, statements with those of others; allegations of Jeb Magruder versus statements of those implicated. Author contends it is all as indigestible as sauerkraut ice cream.

310 July 6, 1973–**U.S. News**, "Watergate's New Chapter: Is Mitchell the Key?" pp. 21-2.
Brings together statements made regarding John Mitchell's involvement or non-involvement in the Watergate affair by Mitchell and by others, including his attorney, presidential counsel J. Fred Buzhardt, John Dean and Martha Mitchell.

311 July 7, 1973–**America**, "Watergate and Pretrial Publicity," Thomas M. Gannon, p. 14.
Details Archibald Cox arguments against televised hearings and committee's rebuttals, and Judge Sirica's ground for pro-committee decision.

312 July 7, 1973–**New Republic**, "Little Things Mean a Lot," TRB, p. 4.
Repeats some of the "smaller" moral lapses connected with forged Kennedy cable, L. Patrick Gray's destruction of E. Howard Hunt papers, hush money and more.

313 July 8, 1973–**New York Times Magazine**, "Richard Nixon's Seventh Crisis," Garry Wills, p. 7+
The April 30 speech failed because Richard Nixon has no clear enemy to blame. Tries to determine why a man who thrives on crisis has failed so miserably in this one.

314   July 9, 1973—**New Yorker**, "Dean's First Day," pp. 22-3.
    Describes the Caucus Room, who is situated where, appearance of committee members, and John Dean's delivery of his opening statement.

315   July 9, 1973—**New Yorker**, "Notes and Comment," p. 21-2.
    Debates how this "law and order" Administration could be so untroubled by moral aspects of Watergate. Speculates about why enemies list and secret police were thought necessary.

316   July 9, 1973—**Newsweek**, "Fallout of Stardom," p. 18.
    How hearings are affecting committee members. How questioning assignments are allotted. Some off-camera fights regarding leaks, pace, immunity related. Attempted White House interference with Senators Howard Baker and Lowell Weicker discussed.

317   July 9, 1973—**Newsweek**, "Portrait of a Presidency," pp. 12-16.
    John Dean's testimony. Dean's points contrasted with presidential statements. White House rebuttals and discrediting attempts reported.

318   July 9, 1973—**Newsweek**, "'There Was a Cancer Growing'," pp. 17-26.
    In-depth reconstruction of John Dean's opening statement and testimony. Cross-examination points. Anti-Dean questions prepared by J. Fred Buzhardt.

319   July 9, 1973—**Newsweek**, "They Had a Little List," pp. 14-15.
    About the "enemies" list: who is on, notes about them, their reactions, weapons to be used against them.

320   July 9, 1973—**Time**, "Awful Lot of Lawyers Involved," Jose M. Ferrer, III, pp. 50-1.
    Talks about possible effects of large number of lawyers involved in Watergate on the legal profession. Examines disbarment procedures, legal ethics.

321   July 9, 1973—**Time**, "Dean's Case Against the President," pp. 6-13.
    New Richard Nixon strategy to blame John Dean and John Mitchell for break-in, John Ehrlichman and H. R. Haldeman for cover-up. Covers Dean's five-day testimony in depth, showing everyone's involvement in cover-up including obstruction of Ervin Committee.

322   July 9, 1973—**Time**, "Hearts and Flowers from John Dean," p. 13.
    Post-hearings interview with John Dean about his feelings, testimony, part in cover-up.

323   July 9, 1973—**Time**, "How to Rehearse for Deception," p. 39.
    John Dean recounting of brainstorming session about how Ron Ziegler should handle questions regarding Dwight Chapin/Donald Segretti dirty tricks, complete with role playing.

324   July 9, 1973—**Time**, "Lowell Weicker Gets Mad," p. 15.
      Lowell Weicker announces Administration attempts to discredit him via implying illegal campaign financing; John Dean says same happened to him. Part of a Weicker/Charles Colson conversation reproduced.

325   July 9, 1973—**Time**, "Playing Politics with Tax Returns," p. 16.
      John Dean alleges attempts to use IRS to get "enemies." Some examples cited. A probe of IRS now being launched under Wilbur Mills' direction.

326   July 9, 1973—**U.S. News**, "Dean's Testimony on Cover-Up: 'The President Was Well Aware of What Had Been Going On'," pp. 14-15.
      Provides portions of the text of John Dean's testimony before the Ervin Committee recounting conversations at meetings he had with Richard Nixon regarding the Watergate affair.

327   July 9, 1973—**U.S. News**, "Nixon's Role in Watergate," pp. 11-13.
      Reports the substance of John Dean's statement and response to questioning before the Ervin Committee regarding the climate which prevailed at the White House and Richard Nixon's role in the cover-up. Inset quotes core of Nixon's May 22 denials.

328   July 11, 1973—**Wall Street Journal**, "One of the 17% Defends Mr. Nixon," Jude Wanniski, p. 12.
      Confronts major surmises that Richard Nixon lied about his part in Watergate affair and does not find John Dean's testimony incriminating to Nixon.

329   July 13, 1973—**Commonweal**, "Role Reversals," p. 370.
      Repeats syndicated columnist Mary McGrory's list of former "good or bad guys" who, in the Watergate context, have switched sides in people's minds.

330   July 13, 1973—**Commonweal**, "Watergate Options," pp. 375-9.
      Suggests the 1972 election could be considered fraudulent because of many illegal activities used to gain votes. Options for contesting the election and possibilities allowed by law for President to be made legally liable given.

331   July 15, 1973—**New York Times Magazine**, "Rap on Zeal," Russell Baker, p. 6.
      Satirical article claims the only crime Waterbuggers will admit to is excessive zeal.

332   July 16, 1973—**Nation**, "'Enemies Project'," p. 34.
      Cautions against thinking enemies list purely amusing. If IRS Commissioner Thrower had not refused to cooperate, it could have had dire consequences.

333   July 16, 1973—**New Yorker**, "Letter from Washington," Richard H. Rovere, pp. 66-70.
      Suggests Richard Nixon may not have understood what John Dean was trying to tell him about staff culpability. Assesses decline in clout with foreign powers.

334   July 16, 1973—**Newsweek**, "'It Never Stops, Does It?'" pp. 21-3.
    Illegal corporate financing under examination. Possible John Mitchell/
Herbert Kalmbach testimony. Purchasing and refurbishing San Clemente under
investigation. Richard Nixon still ignores Watergate and makes no statement.

335   July 16, 1973—**Newsweek**, "Kalmbach's Story," pp. 23-5.
    Herbert Kalmbach to link John Ehrlichman with hush money, H. R. Haldeman
to Tony Ulasewicz money, and John Dean/John Mitchell to raising more hush
money. Testimony in detail—history of fund raising and passing of monies.

336   July 16, 1973—**Newsweek**, "Watergate Mini-Columns," Stewart Alsop, p. 96.
    Disagrees with Gore Vidal's downgrading of America versus Europe. Does
feel an increasing tendency to treat presidents like kings.

337   July 16, 1973—**Time**, "Giving the American Way," p. 10.
    Discusses illegal corporation campaign contributions, notably American Air-
lines, to '72 GOP fund.

338   July 16, 1973—**Time**, "John Mitchell Takes the Stand," pp. 9-10.
    What John Mitchell has been accused of by other witnesses and his probable
responses and testimony.

339   July 16, 1973—**Time**, "Learning to Live with the Scandal," pp. 11-12.
    Describes how the families of those gaining Watergate notoriety are coping
with it.

340   July 16, 1973—**Time**, "Nixon's Lawyers," pp. 16-17.
    Brief biographies of Richard Nixon's two lawyers, J. Fred Buzhardt and
Leonard Garment, along with an explanation of the difficulties of their job.

341   July 16, 1973—**Time**, "Other Investigator," pp. 71-3.
    What Archibald Cox is checking into: Watergate; dirty tricks; illegal contribu-
tions; plumbers; ITT. Brief mention of his staffers' qualifications, his work routine
and expenditures.

342   July 21, 1973—**America**, "White House Homily—Undelivered," pp. 22-3.
    In sermon form, denies private subversion for personal ends equal to public
demonstrations. Condemns Administration for righteous mentality that holds itself
above the law. Calls for open, non-partisan presidency to restore national faith.

343   July 21, 1973—**New Republic**, "Has Nixon Had It?" p. 1+
    Editorial repeats Richard Nixon claims of no knowledge of cover-up but
doubts he could be as uninformed as stated. If so, why did he not demand information? Examines White House horrors and other pre-Watergate illegalities, handling
of L. Patrick Gray, fund disbursements, failure to turn all donation information over
to GAO, how homes were purchased and improved, tax deduction on papers and
gifts.

344 July 21, 1973—**New Republic**, "Watergate Miseries," John Osborne, pp. 16-18.
Richard Nixon problems compound with purchase of homes, improvements on them. Nixon more isolated than ever. Expressions of his private reactions to Watergate developments can only be taken with a grain of salt. Purported current reactions cited and commented on.

345 July 22, 1973—**New York Times Magazine**, "Story So Far," J. Anthony Lukas, p. 1+
Outlines how CREEP was set up when Richard Nixon ostensibly disengaged himself from politics.

346 July 23, 1973—**New Yorker**, "Notes and Comment," pp. 21-2.
Records foreign reactions to Watergate, especially that of Richard Crossman in the *London Times*. Advocates a bit more isolation as the only cure for the authoritarianism rampant in the U.S.

347 July 23, 1973—**Newsweek**, "Following the Footprints of 'Rose Mary's Baby'," p. 20.
List of secret contributors in Rose Mary Woods' possession now under investigation and may lead to prosecution for many business executives. Potential funding-related testimony mentioned.

348 July 23, 1973—**Newsweek**, "Mitchell's 'White House Horrors'," pp. 18-23.
John Mitchell's testimony fails to involve President but shows him to have been oddly incurious. Contrasts with others' stories. Some of the cross-examination on questionable points given. Also testimony of Richard Moore, an extremely hazy refutation of John Dean.

349 July 23, 1973—**Newsweek**, "Stress Test—Who's Lying?" p. 19.
Psychological Stress Evaluator can determine by voice when a person is under stress. Results for John Mitchell, H. R. Haldeman, Charles Colson, and John Dean.

350 July 23, 1973—**Newsweek**, "Toughing It Out," Stewart Alsop, p. 76.
After John Dean testimony, Richard Nixon has nowhere to go but up. John Mitchell and Richard Moore lend slight credibility to uninformed President story. After main witnesses, Nixon will go to public and justify self. Other reasons why he will serve out his term presented.

351 July 23, 1973—**Time**, "And Much More Yet to Come," pp. 23-7.
Goes over expected testimony of Herbert Kalmbach regarding use of campaign funds; John Ehrlichman regarding plumbers, hush money; H. R. Haldeman; and Gordon Strachan. Use of campaign funds to buy San Clemente being examined.

352 July 23, 1973—**Time**, "Backstage with the Ervin Panel," p. 18.
Describes work of behind-the-scenes staff working with the Committee—collecting evidence and screening witnesses.

353   July 23, 1973—**Time**, "Mitchell: 'What Nixon Doesn't Know. . . .'" pp. 16-23.
John Mitchell's testimony shows he withheld information from Richard Nixon
and Nixon did not inquire very far. Claimed to have rejected G. Gordon Liddy plan.
Details conflict between Nixon and his own previous statements and others' state-
ments. Lists the "White House Horrors." Covers cross-examination by Committee.
Also testimony of Richard A. Moore.

354   July 23, 1973—**U.S. News**, "Watergate: Who's Telling the Truth?" pp. 19-21.
Reviews highlights of John Mitchell's testimony before the Ervin Committee
and points out major conflicts between his story and those of Jeb Magruder and
John Dean before the committee.

355   July 26, 1973—**Wall Street Journal**, "Why Nixon Said 'No' on the Tapes,"
      Fred L. Zimmerman, p. 14.
Rationale presented by an anonymous White House official for the President's
decision not to release the recordings of White House conversations to the Ervin
Committee.

356   July 27, 1973—**Commonweal**, "Moral Issue," p. 395.
While the hearings tend to glorify perfectly ordinary senators, they do offer
the chance for America to examine its moral character.

357   July 27, 1973—**Commonweal**, "Watergate: Capital Punishment," Wes
      Barthelmes, pp. 399-403.
Examines possible impact of Watergate on: future elections, future of
Richard Nixon, future of the FBI and CIA, congressional initiative, and campaign
funding reform.

358   July 27, 1973—**Commonweal**, "Watergate: Nixon's Secret Storm," Michael
      Murray, pp. 404-5.
Illustrates why the televised hearings have proven so effective.

359   July 28, 1973—**New Republic**, "Cloak of Immunity," Nathan Lewin,
      pp. 17-18.
Discussion of precedents, possible implications of presidential immunity
claims. Author feels same application for Congress and President should be used.

360   July 28, 1973—**New Republic**, "Drippings from the Watergate," Walter
      Pincus, pp. 10-13.
Richard Moore, special presidential counsel, tells how White House defense
statements are manufactured around the truth, deliberately misunderstanding the
questions and tricky use of words. Herbert Kalmbach testifies campaign money
used for financing George Wallace opponent and investigations rather than
re-election.

361   July 30, 1973—**Los Angeles Times**.
Believes Congress should give serious attention to proposals that would
decrease dependence on private contributors in elections.

362 July 30, 1973—**Nation,** "Miasmas of Watergate: The Truth Is Bad Enough,"
    Ron Dorfman, pp. 73-5.
Watergate paranoia has led to other wild allegations of conspiracies and
cover-ups in leftist press, including sabotage of plane carrying Mrs. E. Howard Hunt.

363 July 30, 1973—**Nation,** "Watergate University," pp. 67-8.
Humorously suggests establishment of a university to study various aspects of
Watergate. Suggests areas of study: women who are involved; political, ethical and
moral aspects; case studies; and new vocabulary terms.

364 July 30, 1973—**New Yorker,** "Notes and Comment," pp. 21-2.
Revelation of bugged White House contradicts Richard Nixon contention of
executive privilege and privacy, since this requested information has been taped for
posterity only. Presidency should be private, not always performing for posterity.
Deplores proposed changes in campaign funding laws.

365 July 30, 1973—**Newsweek,** "Big Oval Sound Studio," p. 17.
Describes possible types and locations of White House bugs, how to detect
tampering with tapes.

366 July 30, 1973—**Newsweek,** "Hindsight Saga," pp. 18-20.
Covers week's hearings, discrepancies with John Mitchell statements. Robert
Mardian felt G. Gordon Liddy told him his authority came direct from Richard
Nixon.

367 July 30, 1973—**Newsweek,** "Nixon Tapes," pp. 12-16.
Richard Nixon refuses to surrender tapes based on executive privilege. Some
possible reasons for this suggested. Origin of bugs and Alexander Butterfield's disclosure covered.

368 July 30, 1973—**Newsweek,** "Teddy White on Watergate," p. 20.
Discusses White's views on effect Watergate and dirty tricks had on 1972 election as seen in his book. Briefly discusses origins of plumbers.

369 July 30, 1973—**Newsweek,** "Who Planted the First Bug?" p. 16.
Delineates bugs from FDR on, foreign reactions, possible "juicy conversations"
about personalities under Richard Nixon that could prove embarrassing.

370 July 30, 1973—**Time,** "Battle for Nixon's Tapes," pp. 7-15.
President refuses to surrender tapes. Reasons why, legal implications, what
they might prove. Recounts history of how existence of tapes was first discovered,
attempts made thus far to obtain them. Discusses why offices bugged, reactions to
it by prominent politicians, which tapes may prove most important. Difficulties in
altering tapes explained.

371 July 30, 1973—**Time**, "How Attorneys Judge the Ervin Hearings," p. 44.
General concensus feels senators have been too soft, failing to follow up inconsistencies, not detailed enough, allow too much rambling. Lists senators' problems or good points as interrogators.

372 July 30, 1973—**Time**, "How Nixon Bugged Himself," p. 10.
Describes set-up of bugs at White House and Executive Office Building, how they were activated, type used.

373 July 30, 1973—**Time**, "Law on the Tapes and Papers," p. 16.
Examines precedents for subpoenaing presidential materials and their applicability in Watergate case.

374 July 30, 1973—**Time**, "Speaking of Money and Propriety," pp. 18-22.
Covers testimony of Herbert Kalmbach about fund raising, hush money; Tony Ulasewicz about money dispersing problems; Frederick LaRue about money dispersements, contradictions of John Mitchell testimony; Robert Mardian, contradicting Mitchell, John Dean and Jeb Magruder and involvement of J. Gordon Liddy; Gordon Strachan, regarding H. R. Haldeman's foreknowledge of intelligence unit.

375 July 30, 1973—**U.S. News**, "Bugging Inside the White House," pp. 16-19.
Presents implications of the disclosure that White House meetings and conversations were recorded and quotes domestic and foreign political leaders on that news. Insets discuss executive privilege and recap testimonies before the Ervin Committee of Herbert Kalmbach, Anthony Ulasewicz, and Frederick LaRue.

376 July 30, 1973—**U.S. News**, "Tales of 'Hush Money'," p. 19.
See *Time*, July 30, "Speaking of Money and Propriety."

377 July 30, 1973—**U.S. News**, "Top Republicans Size Up Impact of Watergate on Their Party," pp. 20-21.
Quotes eleven senators and representatives from various wings of the Republican Party on their impressions of Watergate's impact on the party.

AUGUST 1973

378 August 1973—**Atlantic**, "Watergate Diary," Elizabeth Drew, pp. 60-70.
Notes of all Washington and Watergate happenings during May 1973 by this correspondent.

379 August 1973—**Harper's**, "Temptation of a Sacred Cow," Lewis H. Hampton pp. 43-6+
Fears the triumph of the Watergate disclosure will lead the press to renewed pressure for shield law passage. Records the author's objections to such a law.

380 August 1973—**Parents Magazine**, "Four Point Program to Save Us from Another Watergate," John W. Gardner, p. 16.
See *Current*, July 1973.

381   August 1973—**Ramparts**, "Gang War Erupts," p. 6+
Satiric retelling of Watergate as an underworld altercation.

382   August 1973—**Ramparts**, "Watergate," pp. 34-5.
Questions why Congressional leaders and media executives decided to make Watergate a national scandal after glossing over many previous ones. Criticizes liberals for torpedoing Richard Nixon scenario without having one of their own to replace it with.

383   August 1973—**Today's Health**, "Psychological Fallout: How Other Professionals See It," p. 19+
Interviews with six of the nation's leading psychologists, psychiatrists, and social scientisits on the effect Watergate is having on the American people.

384   August 1973—**Today's Health**, "Therapy to Heal America's Wounded Psyche," pp. 17-19.
Interview with Gunnar Myrdal on why Watergate occurred, and what its effects are on the United States.

385   August 1, 1973—**Washington Post**.
Describes John Ehrlichman's testimony before Senate Watergate Committee and questions United States government's perception in conduct of foreign affairs when unable to see for a year what was going on in White House inner councils.

386   August 3, 1973—**National Review**, "Massa Sam Drives 'Em to the Dictionary," Robert Moses, p. 822.
Questions whether denigrating Richard Nixon will help the United States. Criticizes those who would adopt the British system of vote of confidence rather than impeachment.

387   August 3, 1973—**Wall Street Journal**.
Asks, like Senator Howard Baker, "What did the President know and when did he know it?" Answers in part that in spite of John Dean's testimony it is still possible the President has been telling the truth.

388   August 3, 1973—**Washington Post**.
Deplores attorney John J. Wilson's allusion to Senator Daniel Inouye as "that little Jap."

389   August 4, 1973—**Washington Post**.
Suggests Ervin Committee and Special Prosecutor Archibald Cox are particularly well positioned to clean up ITT antitrust case in which whole Administration Watergate cast seems involved.

390   August 6, 1973—**Newsweek**, "Dueling Solons: Nixon's Powers," p. 20.
Recounts arguments of Sam Ervin and John J. Wilson during the hearings about the extent of presidential powers.

391   August 6, 1973—**Newsweek**, "Ehrlichman Hangs Tough," pp. 18-26.
Summarizes John Ehrlichman's testimony before the Ervin Committee, including his rationale for the Ellsberg burglary. Highlights contradictions between his assertions and those of other witnesses.

392   August 6, 1973—**Newsweek**, "Man behind the Subpoena," p. 16.
Outlines the various aspects of Watergate that Special Prosecutor Archibald Cox is investigating. Cox's current life-style described.

393   August 6, 1973—**Newsweek**, "Need (Not) to Know," Shana Alexander, p. 31.
Questions the Administration for operating on a "need to know" or "need not to know" basis. Not only was information withheld from aides, but they never inquired any deeper than they felt necessary.

394   August 6, 1973—**Newsweek**, "Showdown," pp. 12-17.
Presents Richard Nixon's reasons for not releasing the tapes to Archibald Cox or the Ervin Committee. Steps taken to obtain the tapes and subsequent refusals retraced. Possible precedents explored.

395   August 6, 1973—**Newsweek**, "Translating Watergate," p. 47.
Describes difficulty foreign correspondents based here have had in relating Watergate to their home readers.

396   August 6, 1973—**Time**, "Battle over Presidential Power," pp. 8-21.
Richard Nixon's refusal to comply with subpoenas arouses constitutional crisis which can only be resolved by Supreme Court. Cites reactions to his refusal, his basis for refusing, past lack of legal precedents, avenues open to Supreme Court.

397   August 6, 1973—**Time**, "Ehrlichman Mentality on View," pp. 22-7.
Examines John Ehrlichman's ethical concepts as shown in his testimony. Lists his answers to previous witnesses' allegations. Three of his own contentions about why Ellsberg burglary necessary rebutted by Committee.

398   August 6, 1973—**Time**, "Ghostly Conversation on the Meaning of Watergate,"
         Stanley Cloud, pp. 14-15.
Fictional discussion between Thomas Jefferson and Alexander Hamilton discussing pros and cons of powerful, alienated presidency versus the public as mob.

399   August 6, 1973—**U.S. News**, "Nixon vs. the Investigators," pp. 11-13.
Details the conflict over the White House tapes between Richard Nixon and Archibald Cox and the Ervin Committee. Explains possible impact of Supreme Court ruling on separation of powers doctrine.

400   August 6, 1973—**U.S. News**, "Watergate Fallout: Government in Disarray,"
         pp. 15-17.
Surveys officials in and out of federal government regarding their views on the effect of Watergate and resultant changes in high level positions on governmental processes.

401   August 8, 1973—**Chicago Tribune**.
Deplores Mr. Agnew's investigation as adding to the troubles of an already beleaguered government, but says something awe-inspiring about judicial arm of government pursuing criminal charges against two top government officials.

402   August 10, 1973—**New York Times**.
Believes some form of public financing is the answer to campaign funding abuse as seen in Watergate but sees many problems, particularly in primaries. Need formulas to protect country against known, extensive and inescapable evils of mixing private money and public politics.

403   August 10, 1973—**Wall Street Journal**, "Sam Young Visits the Home Folks," Albert R. Hunt, p. 6.
A freshman Republican congressman from Illinois visits his constituents and is faced with possible effects of the Watergate revelations on his reelection bid.

404   August 10, 1973—**Washington Post**.
A brighter picture for public TV beginning with prime-time coverage of Watergate hearings.

405   August 11, 1973—**Christian Science Monitor**.
Comments on Spiro Agnew resignation. If that happens United States would have first experience under new amendment to the Constitution covering succession. Question is—who would Richard Nixon nominate? Meanwhile, political implications of Watergate in background.

406   August 11, 1973—**New York Times**.
Spiro Agnew compares his position to that of President Richard Nixon— immune from indictment, prosecution or even testimony—an extension of argument that Mr. Nixon can be tried in the courts for crimes only after impeached, convicted and removed from office.

407   August 11, 1973—**Washington Post**.
Watergate lessons for the legal profession: congratulates American Bar Association on moves at convention to offset bad reputation lawyers have earned by so many being involved in Watergate.

408   August 12, 1973—**Denver Post**.
Sees cloud over Nixon presidency—not only unproved suspicions concerning Watergate but also strong indication the President has been using his powers and allowing others to use his powers in ways that evade the law.

409   August 12, 1973—**Washington Post**.
Comments on barbaric idiom in which Nixon men communicated, and how this abuse of language was used to cover up wrong-doing by making it seem right. (Newspeak?)

410   August 13, 1973—**Nation**, "Double Standard Shoe," pp. 98-9.
Contrasts conduct of the Ervin Committee with the Army-McCarthy hearings.

411 August 13, 1973–**Nation**, "Response to an Insiders' Coup D'Etat," Michael
        Reisman, p. 102.
     Calls Watergate a coup d'etat; examines various methods of remedying an
illegal election.

412 August 13, 1973–**New Yorker**, "Notes and Comment," pp. 21-2.
     Feels the course of the hearings has been influenced by the witnesses–i.e., ques-
tions asked were slanted by John Dean's testimony accusing Nixon, and by John
Mitchell's separation of the White House from CREEP. A more important question
is whether the whole Administration committed illegal acts.

413 August 13, 1973–**Time**, "Battle for Those Tapes Begins," pp. 8-9.
     White House lawyers deliver brief to Judge Sirica arguing why tapes should
not be surrendered. Pro and con arguments presented, along with public opinion on
the subject.

414 August 13, 1973–**Time**, "Counterattack and Counterpoint," pp. 9-17.
     H. R. Haldeman's testimony delineated, including his rendition of the two
tapes he heard of conversations with John Dean and compares with Dean testimony.
Moves on to Richard Helms' and General Vernon Walters' testimony; also that of
Robert Cushman and L. Patrick Gray.

415 August 13, 1973–**U.S. News**, "Watergate: The President's Men Speak Out in
        His Defense," pp. 21-3.
     See *Time*, August 13, "Counterattack and Counterpoint."

416 August 13, 1973–**Washington Post**.
     Questions how well the courts will serve the nation in the Archibald Cox and
Senate Watergate Committee cases–will they grasp the constitutional questions
involved or try to duck the issues by finding procedural irregularity in one or both
cases?

417 August 17, 1973–**National Review**, "Presidential Tapes," William F. Buckley,
        pp. 910-11.
     Discusses whether Richard Nixon should have taped conversations and how
legal the executive privilege plea is.

418 August 17, 1973–**National Review**, "Watergate and the Election," pp. 879-80.
     Goes over various dramatic, ironic aspects of Watergate, along with leftward
trend of recent legislation.

419 August 17, 1973–**New York Times**.
     Wonders if the public really believes the President has learned anything from
Watergate when he displays so little recognition that his high-ranking aides gravely
distorted concepts of individual freedom in the name of "security."

420   August 17, 1973—**Washington Post**.
Comments on President Richard Nixon's televised speech and finds the whole array of misplaced blame disheartening and of a piece with his air of personal detachment.

421   August 19, 1973—**Washington Post**.
Refutes Richard Nixon's observation that elected officials, meaning Congress, should put Watergate behind them and get on with the nation's business by enumerating congressional actions during Senate Watergate hearings.

422   August 20, 1973—**New Yorker**, "Notes and Comment," pp. 21-2.
Decries Harris poll results showing 69% feel dirty campaign practices are rampant in each party. Alleges this attitude the same as under a dictatorship. Feels Watergate a result of national corruption that culminated in the Vietnam War.

423   August 20, 1973—**Time**, "Watergate 1: The Evidence to Date," pp. 16-18.
Synopsizes evidence from hearings on: 1970 intelligence plan, Ellsberg burglary, plumbers, CIA and FBI misuse, executive clemency, hush money, destruction of records, G. Gordon Liddy plans, and overtures to Judge Byrne.

424   August 20, 1973—**Time**, "Witnesses to a Spreading Stain," pp. 14-5.
Final witnesses' testimony given: L. Patrick Gray, Richard Kleindienst, and Henry Petersen, all of whom spoke of White House interference in the investigation and prosecution of the case.

425   August 20, 1973—**U.S. News**, "Effect of Watergate: 'Far More Political Than Legal'," pp. 50-2.
Interview with Senator Howard Baker on the aims of the Ervin Committee, tapes issue, lessons emerging from both the hearings and Watergate itself.

426   August 20, 1973—**U.S. News**, "Phase 1 of Watergate Ends—Now It's Nixon's Turn," pp. 48-50.
Summarizes testimony given in final sessions of the Ervin Committee's initial phase of investigation and outlines the grounds for the legal struggle between Special Prosecutor Archibald Cox and the White House over presidential tapes.

427   August 20, 1973—**U.S. News**, "Prosecutor vs. President: The Role of Archibald Cox," p. 47.
Defines role of special prosecutor as seen by Archibald Cox. Mentions five task forces reporting to him. Some anecdotal and biographical material.

428   August 20, 1973—**U.S. News**, "'Serious Threat to the Presidency'," p. 49.
Excerpt from the brief presented by Richard Nixon attorneys explaining why tapes should not be surrendered.

429   August 22, 1973—**Washington Post**.
Burden rests with Department of Justice to ensure its responsibilities are carried out, especially in wake of Watergate.

430 August 24, 1973–**Christian Science Monitor.**
Responds to President Richard Nixon's press conference at San Clemente. Believes polls will show favorable response and that by accepting tough leading Watergate questions he has brought himself back into touch with the American people.

431 August 24, 1973–**Commonweal,** "Hearings Overcovered?" p. 442.
Presents remarks of radio commentator Elizabeth Drew criticizing excessive press covering of the hearings.

432 August 24, 1973–**Washington Post.**
Expects the case of the Constitution and the Richard Nixon tapes to go to the Supreme Court to determine the extent to which the presidency is circumscribed.

433 August 26, 1973–**Washington Post.**
Sees President Nixon's ideas of executive privilege increasing with each new demand of Watergate tapes as opposed to what Americans generally understand as the balance of power.

434 August 27, 1973–**Nation,** "Contemptible Triumvirate," Carey McWilliams, p. 130-5.
Traces background that led to Watergate and the cover-up. Presents H. R. Haldeman's testimony, accenting his account of presidential tapes' contents. John Ehrlichman's part in Watergate examined. Calls for massive rejection by the public of the Nixon-Haldeman-Ehrlichman triumvirate.

435 August 27, 1973–**New Yorker,** "Notes and Comment," pp. 19-20.
Examines Richard Nixon's recent address, showing how various statements are misleading or incorrect.

436 August 27, 1973–**Newsweek,** "Key Questions," pp. 18-20.
Richard Nixon's latest speech quoted along with facts gleaned thus far on: Ellsberg burglary, Watergate break-in, when he learned the truth, initial investigation, hush money and clemency, and past cover-up.

437 August 27, 1973–**Newsweek,** "Making of a Silent Minority," pp. 14-17.
Background of Richard Nixon's latest speech and his failure to once again divulge the entire truth described.

438 August 27, 1973–**Time,** "Scrambling to Break Clear of Watergate," pp. 11-14.
Concentrates on background to Richard Nixon's latest speech, as well as capsulizing its contents and reaction to it.

439 August 27, 1973–**Time,** "Watergate: The View from Jail," pp. 18-21.
Howard Hunt's reaction to the mushrooming disclosures of Watergate. Deals with his bitterness on his own treatment as well as compared to others involved.

440   August 27, 1973—**U.S. News**, "Even the President 'Is Subject to the Rule of Law'," p. 83.
Excerpts from the brief filed by Special Prosecutor Archibald Cox requesting the presidential tapes.

441   August 27, 1973—**U.S. News**, "Is Worst Over for Nixon?" pp. 14-16.
See *Time*, August 27, "Scrambling to Break Clear of Watergate."

442   August 27, 1973—**U.S. News**, "Nixon's Address to Nation on the Watergate Case," pp. 77-80.
Complete text of Richard Nixon's August 15 address.

443   August 27, 1973—**U.S. News**, "President's Written Statement," pp. 81-3.
Text of the statement issued jointly with the August 15 address.

444   August 28, 1973—**Washington Post**.
Compares previous undercover activities and draws line from them to Watergate.

445   August 30, 1973—**Los Angeles Times**.
Suggests the President should voluntarily surrender tapes to the courts, thus maintaining executive privilege and mitigating a constitutional confrontation.

446   August 31, 1973—**Washington Post**.
Order of Judge Sirica for White House tapes leads to discussion as a landmark case on presidential privilege.

SEPTEMBER 1973

447   Autumn 1973—**American Scholar**, "Watergate: One End, But Which?" Gerald W. Johnson, pp. 594-603.
Criticizes majority who elected Richard Nixon and thereby paved the way for Watergate, but ameliorates this by showing how the public was kept in ignorance, particularly about Vietnam. Feels Watergate will either add to national insecurity or jolt us into readjustment.

448   September, 1973—**Commentary**, "Appointment with Watergate," Seymour Martin Lipset and Earl Raab, pp. 35-43.
Traces history of radical movements in America that led to repressive backlashes. Shows how Richard Nixon's background made him anti-conspiracy leader and how White House atmosphere led to Watergate.

449   September 1973—**Harper's**, "As the Watergate Turns," p. 58.
Speculates as to why Ervin Committee hearings are not more popular: reminds people of instability in life, people desire somnolence, and belief that none of committee members believes in the integrity of his own position.

450 September-October 1973—**Society**, "Social Scientists Speak on Watergate,"
    pp. 15-27.
Contains statements of six social scientists on various aspects of Watergate:
Edward Schneier, Murray Weidenbaum, Herbert Marcuse, Ithiel de Sola Pool,
Robert Nisbet, and Stuart Umpleby.

451 September 3, 1973—**Chicago Tribune**.
Finds it distressing that men like James McCord and Jeb Magruder have gall
to plan series of college lectures for fat fees. Expects Judge Sircia to rule these
personal appearances out of order.

452 September 3, 1973—**Nation**, "Nixon Mire," pp. 162-3.
Examines reasons why Richard Nixon dare not release the tapes—H. R.
Haldeman and John Ehrlichman can then subpoena and when refused, move for
dismissal. Holds Nixon violated so-called confidentiality by recording in the first
place. Problems facing Nixon that are also eroding his power mentioned.

453 September 3, 1973—**New Yorker**, "Notes and Comment," pp. 19-21.
States President's claim of executive immunity regarding the tapes places him
above the law. Deplores the fact that public must rely on leaks, since truth has not
been forthcoming any other way. Asserts that publicity will not adversely influence
trials.

454 September 3, 1973—**Newsweek**, "Historic Duel for the Nixon Tapes," p. 37.
Presents claims of White House for not releasing tapes and Archibald Cox
arguments for submitting them as presented to Judge Sirica.

455 September 3, 1973—**Newsweek**, "On the Rebound?" pp. 22-6.
Reviews reasons for Richard Nixon holding recent news conference. Presents
his answers to some press questions.

456 September 3, 1973—**Time**, "Savage Game of Twenty Questions," pp. 10-11.
Excerpts questions and answers of Richard Nixon's August 22 press conference.

457 September 3, 1973—**Time**, "Struggle for Nixon's Tapes," pp. 29-33.
Synopsizes most important points pro and con turning presidential tapes over
as presented orally in Judge Sirica's court.

458 September 7, 1973—**Commonweal**, "They Went to College," pp. 467-8.
Cites indications that higher education is being blamed for Watergate, and
praised for producing people associated with the hearings.

459 September 7, 1973—**Commonweal**, "Watergate and Civil Disobedience,"
    Peter Steinfels, p. 470.
Analyzes the comparison of those participating in Watergate with those who
engaged in civil disobedience made by President Richard Nixon.

460 September 7, 1973—**Washington Post**.
Under pressure from Watergate Special Prosecutor Archibald Cox are officers of at least seven major corporations who admit making illegal contributions to Richard Nixon campaign.

461 September 8, 1973—**America**, "Watergate Honeymoon," S. J. Adamo,
       pp. 152-3.
Press now criticizing itself for active participation in hearings rather than merely recording them. Press leaks condemned. Calls for responsibility in future coverage.

462 September 8, 1973—**New Republic**, "Loose Ends," Walter Pincus, pp. 19-21.
Delineates loose ends he feels new session of Ervin Committee should tie up: Who will investigate White House fund? Who called J. Gordon Liddy and told him to contact Richard Kleindienst? How and when did other major figures hear of Watergate? What was the content of Nixon-Haldeman-Ehrlichman meeting on June 20, 1972?

463 September 8, 1973—**New Republic**, "Sirica Decision," pp. 7-9.
In-depth examination of Judge Sirica's tape decision and where it falls short of being definitive in permitting further appeals.

464 September 10, 1973—**New Yorker**, "Notes and Comment," pp. 31-2.
Feels President at an advantage in a press conference as to what and how he will answer, so White House euphoria over latest one unfounded. Attempts to evade or lie will eventually come out.

465 September 10, 1973—**Newsweek**, "War for the Nixon Tapes," pp. 19-22.
Presents bases for Judge Sirica's decision that Richard Nixon must relinquish the tapes and how they should be previewed. Reactions to it capsulized. Possible future White House strategy mentioned.

466 September 10, 1973—**Time**, "Highlights of Judge Sirica's Decision," p. 17.
Excerpts of Judge Sirica's decision on the release of the presidential tapes.

467 September 10, 1973—**Time**, "Judge Commands the President," pp. 14-16.
Judge Sirica's main points in finding against Richard Nixon listed, along with several options he has regarding the censoring of the tapes. No decision as yet on Ervin Committee request for tapes, but White House position repeated.

468 September 10, 1973—**Time**, "People's Verdict Is In," pp. 18-19.
Results of *Time* poll as to credibility of President, John Dean, H. R. Haldeman, John Ehrlichman, and John Mitchell.

469 September 10, 1973—**U.S. News**, "Judge Sirica: Courts, Not the President,
       Must Decide if Tapes Are 'Privileged'," p. 16.
See *Time*, September 10, "Highlights of Judge Sirica's Decision."

470 September 10, 1973—**U.S. News**, "Watergate: Now the Courts Move In,"
     pp. 15-17.
     Aside from Judge Sirica's decision, details other court battles and trials relating to Watergate. Mentioned latest opinion poll responses to hearings and televised coverage. Lists "dirty tricks" to be investigated.

471 September 10, 1973—**Washington Post**.
     Comments on lack of interest of TV networks to televise second set of Senate Watergate hearings and the right of the people to know what really went on, paid for by their money.

472 September 11, 1973—**Wall Street Journal**, "Watergate and the Political
     Pendulum," Jude Wanniski, p. 20.
     Argues that the Republican Party and political movement Richard Nixon led are still intact despite revelations concerning Watergate.

473 September 12, 1973—**Christian Century**, "Needed: Leadership, Not Deception," pp. 875-6.
     Examines two types of fallacious arguments used to explain away Watergate by trying to relate two unrelated things, such as Watergate and war protests. Calls for straight language instead of these fallacies.

474 September 14, 1973—**National Review**, "Unmentionable Uses of a CIA,"
     Miles Copeland, pp. 990-97.
     Majority of the article devoted to CIA duties and activities, with brief mention of how White House tried to involve it in Watergate and subsequent cover-up. Personal reminiscences about Howard Hunt and James McCord included.

475 September 15, 1973—**New Republic**, "Forgive and Forget?" pp. 5-6.
     Questions whether investigations, both official and press, are grinding to a halt. Suggests new areas of inquiry based on recent information: ITT, bugging of newsmen, CIA, size of White House staff, and making leaks illegal.

476 September 15, 1973—**New Republic**, "Shades of Meaning," John Osborne,
     pp. 10-12.
     Contrasts contradicting statements of Richard Nixon and Clark MacGregor on Nixon request to investigate whether any CREEP member was involved in Watergate, and White House non-involvment in the campaign. Early Jeb Magruder statement supports MacGregor's story.

477 September 15, 1973—**Washington Post**.
     Comments on common sense plan by Court of Appeals in permitting the President and Special Prosecutor Archibald Cox to come to an agreement over tapes before the court is forced to decide and perhaps stretch the Constitution to intolerable limits.

478 September 16, 1973—**New York Times**.
     Discusses tapes and the President's assertion that he alone should decide which should go to grand jury. Believes it rare that defendants in a criminal case

can claim they discussed matter with President of United States, and that executive privilege was never intended to be shield for wrongdoing.

479   September 17, 1973–**Time**, "Confused Alarms of Struggle," pp. 22-3.
      As time in which usefulness of tapes diminishes, Archibald Cox and Sam Ervin race to get them while White House appeals Judge Sirica's decision. Cox asks tapes be given directly to him without Sirica first censoring. Offers Richard Nixon's replies to questions about whether he will comply with this or Supreme Court decision.

480   September 17, 1973–**U.S. News**, "Rush Toward Judgment in Watergate Case," pp. 33-4.
      Latest court developments: California grand jury indicts four aides in Ellsberg burglary; federal grand jury moves toward indictments; trial to begin for John Mitchell and Maurice Stans in Vesco case. Public reaction in letters to congressmen reported. Tapes controversy now rests with appellate court.

481   September 19, 1973–**Christian Century**, "Executive Privilege and Judicial Prerogatives," J. Claude Evans, pp. 910-11.
      Examines past interpretations of executive privilege, including a paper by Paul Hardin, III. Conclusions support Judge Sirica's decision.

482   September 20, 1973–**Philadelphia Inquirer**.
      Declines to generalize but feels it folly to ignore the fact that over all Watergate proceedings hangs the simple question: whether the criminal justice system in the United States prevails over men in power or is prevailed over by them.

483   September 21, 1973–**Commonweal**, "Hypocrisy in Action," p. 490.
      Lists misleading statements of Ron Ziegler and Richard Nixon regarding Watergate.

484   September 23, 1973–**Washington Post**.
      Suggests that Richard Nixon is gravely complicating the process which offers the most hope of restoring the moral and political authority of his office.

485   September 24, 1973–**Newsweek**, "Nixon's Tapes: How to Settle out of Court," pp. 33-5.
      Describes compromise plan to let Archibald Cox decide which tape portions applicable while Richard Nixon retains authority over them. Ervin Committee cuts back on the hearings. Several Watergate indictees attempt to obtain appropriate tapes for their trials.

486   September 24, 1973–**Time**, "Forgotten Cubans," p. 26.
      Four Cubans imprisoned grow increasingly bitter about being used, being lumped with those who really knew what was going on, and undetermined length of their sentences.

487   September 24, 1973–**Time**, "Tough Guy," pp. 24-5.

Examines grounds for possible indictment of Charles Colson in Ellsberg break-in. Lists "dirty tricks" Colson may have been involved in.

488   September 24, 1973–**U.S. News**, "Watergate: A Move to Avert a Nixon-vs.-Court Showdown," p. 35.

Presents the compromise that Richard Nixon, lawyer Charles Alan Wright, and Archibald Cox screen tapes and decide which are applicable. New Ervin Committee schedule given.

489   September 26, 1973–**Christian Century**, "Watergate: Religious Issues and Answers," pp. 937-42.

Answers of twenty-two religious leaders to the question: what is the central religious or theological issue posed by Watergate and how will we as a people find resources to deal with this issue?

490   September 27, 1973–**Christian Science Monitor**.

Takes as premise the doctrine that in the United States only the people are sovereign and that no man is above the law–Spiro Agnew or Richard Nixon–vice-president or president.

491   September 27, 1973–**New York Times**.

Says Mr. Spiro Agnew as citizen is innocent until proven otherwise, but as a potential president must be above suspicion. In the event of transfer of presidential power in an emergency such a risk as Agnew is unacceptable.

492   September 28, 1973–**National Review**, "Back to Normalcy," p. 1038.

Unwillingness of those investigating to suggest a conclusion to Watergate–i.e., impeachment, has led to impatience and boredom of public. Feels ship of state will still sail under these conditions, albeit somewhat slower.

493   September 28, 1973–**Washington Post**.

Comments that after five months of Watergate hearings, the purpose of the Committee is not to punish by exposure past misdeeds by Republicans–it is to prevent future corruption by writing new legislation.

494   September 29, 1973–**Business Week**, "How Watergate Paralyzes Policy," p. 32.

Illustrates how White House failure to act on various domestic crises indicates their preoccupation with Watergate. Urges Richard Nixon to turn problems over to Cabinet. If they cannot cope, get new members who can.

495   September 29, 1973–**New Republic**, "Tapes, Cox, Nixon," Alexander M. Bickel, pp. 13-14.

Contends that since Prosecutor Archibald Cox is a subordinate of President Nixon, Nixon can fire him at any time. Feels tapes case must be dismissed because it is not the court's job to decide litigation between President and himself in guise of a subordinate. Discusses potential jobs of the grand jury.

496   September 29, 1973—**New York Times**.
   Regrets that Senate Watergate Committee had neither the will nor sophistica-
tion to challenge contemptible diversionary tactics at hearings, linking major founda-
tions to "dirty tricks" and publication of *Quicksilver Times*, according to Patrick J.
Buchanan a radical underground newspaper.

497   September 30, 1973—**Los Angeles Times**.
   Discusses the question of power and its use. Actions of Watergate defendants
and Judge Sirica all go to the question of government power in any era from the
authority of the President, Congress, courts, and on down the scale.

OCTOBER 1973

498   October 1973—**Current**, "Meaning of Watergate," pp. 3-29.
   Excerpts articles by: Stanley Cloud, *Time*, August 6, 1973; Hans Morgen-
thau, *New Republic*, August 11, 1973; Ramsey Clark, *Nation*, June 4, 1973;
editors, *Ramparts*, August-September 1973; Arthur Kinoy, a speech, July 5, 1973;
editors, *New Yorker*, August 20, 1973; Barbara Tuchman, *New York Times*,
August 10, 1973. The starred items are annotated in this bibliography.

499   October 1973—**Harper's**, "Grand Inquest of the Nation," Raoul Berger,
      pp. 12-23.
   Cites congressional records to prove that executive privilege is a myth without
the constitutional basis which Richard Nixon claims it has. Protests that Nixon's
withholding of information denies Congress' role as inquisitor and is a perversion
of the separation of powers.

500   October 1973—**Harper's**, "Reflections on a Course in Ethics," Studs Terkel,
      p. 59.
   Discussion between Jeb Magruder and former teacher William Sloan Coffin
regarding their college days, why they got involved pro- or anti-government, how
Watergate happened, and release of the Pentagon Papers.

501   October 1973—**Notre Dame Lawyer**, "Electronic Eavesdropping: A Victim's
      Primer," pp. 162-84.
   Surveys the major case law on the subject of electronic surveillance and
reviews current statutory prohibitions against illicit eavesdropping. Refers to the
Watergate and Ellsberg cases and recommends that available sanctions for the dis-
regard of the law be applied at every opportunity.

502   October 1973—**Ramparts**, "Inside Look: Watergate and the World of the CIA,"
      L. Fletcher Prouty, pp. 21-3+
   In-depth discussion of history, organization and operation of CIA. Shows that
CIA methods were suggested for Huston plan, used by plumbers.

503   October 1, 1973—**Newsweek**, ". . . And Watergate Simmers On," pp. 31-2.
   Explains proposals of Archibald Cox and White House to each other regarding
access to tapes and why they took these stances. Previews E. Howard Hunt's

testimony, which will involve Charles Colson. Attempt of Watergate Five to reverse their pleas may elicit new information.

504   October 1, 1973—**Newsweek**, "Breaking from the Gate," pp. 103-4.
Summarizes a few of the entries in the race to publish Watergate exposés.

505   October 8, 1973—**Newsweek**, "Good News," Liz Carpenter, pp. 24-5.
Shares views of people around the country on Watergate. Lists good effects—particularly increased involvement of people in politics.

506   October 8, 1973—**Newsweek**, "Hard-Nosed Lesson in Politics," pp. 36-42.
Repeats speechwriter Pat Buchanan's fiery testimony, lambasting Committee for leaks, short notice on his appearance, and strongly denying Watergate involvement. E. Howard Hunt's new testimony implicating Charles Colson repeated.

507   October 11, 1973—**Denver Post**.
In light of Spiro Agnew resignation under criminal charges, the country needs a person acceptable to Congress and respected by the American people who disagree with him. Feels Mr. Nixon will easily find such a person within Republican ranks.

508   October 11, 1973—**New York Times**.
Believes Spiro Agnew personal tragedy is part of larger tragedy of the Nixon Administration, overwhelmingly reelected and now daily beset by fresh scandal, looked on by the public in mingled shame and dismay.

509   October 11, 1973—**Washington Post**.
Denies Vice President Agnew has been made scapegoat for Watergate.

510   October 14, 1973—**Los Angeles Times**.
Considers President's defense of principle of executive privilege has been stretched to absurdity. Definition of separation of powers left imprecise. Its resolution must be left to experience—and in no way is the President above and beyond the reaches of the law and the Constitution.

511   October 14, 1973—**New York Times**.
Sees no justification for Mr. Nixon's claim that Judge Sirica's order for tapes threatens "the continued existence of the Presidency as a functioning institution." The true threat is lingering suspicion that presidential privilege is being abused in effort to interfere with processes of criminal justice.

512   October 14, 1973—**Washington Post**.
Considers Court of Appeals decision wise that recognizes executive privilege but says that interests that would be served by withholding information from Watergate tapes had to be balanced against those who would be served by the disclosure.

513   October 15, 1973—**New Yorker**, "Letter from Washington," Richard H.
         Rovere, pp. 170-7.
    Traces Richard Nixon's political career briefly, trying to ascertain why he
appointed business and advertising men as aides rather than politicians.

514   October 15, 1973—**U.S. News**, "Watergate: Tapes Issue Nears Showdown,"
         p. 25.
    Presents Richard Nixon's stand refusing to compromise in the tapes issue.
Ervin Committee's right to the tapes also challenged. Donald Segretti's testimony
before the Committee summarized. The four Cubans imprisoned petition for
retrial.

515   October 15, 1973—**Washington Post**.
    Questions the gift of $100,000 cash from Howard Hughes to Mr. Rebozo;
what the Richard Nixon-Hughes relationship really is; and its part in the Committee
to Reelect the President.

516   October 17, 1973—**Wall Street Journal**, "Thinking Things Over: The Public
         Morality," Vermont Royster, p. 20.
    Compares Spiro Agnew's illegal activities with Watergate because both assume
"everyone is doing it," therefore it is all right. Praises public for condemning both.

517   October 20, 1973—**Business Week**, "Triple Threat to Illegal Givers," pp. 33-4.
    Recapitulates companies fined for illegal political contributions. Other com-
panies Special Prosecutor Archibald Cox is checking out enumerated. Ervin Committee trying to find out how and why illegal contributions were made, how the
law should be changed, and what effect such changes could have.

518   October 21, 1973—**Washington Post**.
    Examines agreements and events that led to Richard Nixon's firing of Chief
Watergate Prosecutor Archibald Cox and subsequent resignation of Attorney
General Elliot Richardson. Calls it "justice undone."

519   October 22, 1973—**Chicago Tribune**.
    Says course Richard Nixon is pursuing is wrong and he has brought a catastro-
phe on himself by firing Archibald Cox and trying to make a deal over Watergate
tapes. Thinks he must seek reconciliation with Congress, courts, and American
people since the United States cannot afford another constitutional crisis.

520   October 22, 1973—**Los Angeles Times**.
    Declares discharge of Special Prosecutor Archibald Cox a breach of the
President's word and a serious mistake that discredits his leadership and perils the
balance of power.

521   October 22, 1973—**New York Times**.
    Feels the weekend debacle starting with the firing of Special Prosecutor
Archibald Cox has brought to light some indication of ways in which the President has been seeking to obstruct the inquiry into the Watergate scandals.

522   October 22, 1973–**New Yorker**, "Notes and Comment," p. 35.
      Senator George McGovern's political director, Frank Mankiewicz, testifies
about the conduct of the campaign. Reports on memos by Pat Buchanan about
dirty tricks to ensure McGovern's candidacy.

523   October 22, 1973–**Newsweek**, "Hughes Connection," p. 52.
      See *Time*, October 22, "Hughes Connection."

524   October 22, 1973–**Newsweek**, "'Law Applies to Every Man'," p. 44.
      Excerpts Appellate Court's decision supporting Judge Sirica.

525   October 22, 1973–**Newsweek**, "Nixon Tapes: Round Two to Cox," pp. 43-4.
      Explains reasons cited by the Appellate Court in supporting Judge Sirica's
decision that the Presidential tapes be surrendered.

526   October 22, 1973–**Time**, "Hughes Connection," pp. 25-6.
      Mentions Ervin Committee investigations into Howard Hughes donation
handled by Bebe Rebozo and Rebozo's purchase of some San Clemente land.
Hearings also go into widespread bipartisan political dirty tricks. Egil Krogh indicted
in the Ellsberg burglary.

527   October 22, 1973–**Time**, "Rejecting Nixon's Absolutes," p. 25.
      See *Newsweek*, October 22, "Nixon Tapes: Round Two to Cox."

528   October 22, 1973–**Washington Post**.
      Assesses the damage done by Richard Nixon as result of Archibald Cox firing
on the institutions over which he was elected to preside.

529   October 22, 1973–**Washington Post**.
      Contends that President's quarrel is not just with the ranking members of the
Watergate Committee or Congress but with the courts whose unambiguous command he seems determined to defy.

530   October 24, 1973–**Washington Post**.
      Thinks there is no more "pressing business" affecting security of United
States than deciding whether Richard Nixon, by his performance across whole
range of Watergate matters, has not proved himself incapable of governing.

531   October 25, 1973–**Washington Post**.
      Deplores absence of Special Prosecutor since Archibald Cox firing and details
special Watergate items since summer of 1972.

532   October 27, 1973–**Business Week**, "Crisis of Double Standards at the Bar,"
      p. 33.
      Condemns bar associations for failing to police their ranks. Those involved in
Watergate seem to feel they have done nothing wrong. Calls them hypocritical,
copping a plea on basis that their fall is punishment enough.

533 October 27, 1973—**Business Week**, "Heat Is Still on the Corporate Givers,"
     p. 34.
Offers suggestions about how to judge effectiveness of new special prosecutor.
Some of Archibald Cox's recent areas of exploration listed, including ITT, milk
fund, and Howard Hughes loan.

534 October 27, 1973—**New Republic**, "Who Gets the Tapes?" Nathan Lewin,
     pp. 14-16.
Examines the upholding of Judge Sirica's decision regarding releasing the
tapes. Faults the Judge for lack of clarity as to how the tapes will be screened. Suggests Richard Nixon may appeal to Supreme Court. Speculates about how Nixon
may pre-screen the tapes before turning them over.

535 October 28, 1973—**St. Louis Post-Dispatch**.
After firing of Archibald Cox, contends that new special prosecutor is needed,
authorized and funded by Congress, and appointed by a court having nothing to do
with hearing the case. Congress has indisputable authority to appoint such an officer
under Article 2 of the Constitution.

536 October 28, 1973—**Washington Post**.
Charges Richard Nixon's view that media reporting of Archibald Cox firing
is "outrageous, vicious, distorted and frantic" can be regarded by a disturbed public as yet another "cover-up" maneuver.

537 October 29, 1973—**Newsweek**, "Great Tapes Crisis," pp. 22-30.
Recounts events of and leading up to the "Saturday Night Massacre" in
which Archibald Cox, Elliot Richardson and William Ruckelshaus were fired or
resigned. Outlines proposed compromise for Senator John Stennis to audit tapes
and pass on relevant ones, which was turned down by Cox and led to firing.

538 October 29, 1973—**Time**, "Ehrlichman's Lib Lawyer," p. 106.
Profiles career of John Ehrlichman's defense lawyer in the Ellsberg burglary,
Joseph A. Ball, who was Anthony Russo's original lawyer. Some of his potential
approaches to the case mentioned, including subpoenaing presidential tapes.

539 October 29, 1973—**Time**, "Richard Nixon Stumbles to the Brink," pp. 12-19.
See *Newsweek*, October 29.

540 October 29, 1973—**U.S. News**, "Nixon's 'Way Out' in Battle of the Tapes,"
     p. 28.
Presents the tapes compromise in which Senator Stennis is to listen to the
tapes and judge whether transcript for Judge Sirica is correct. Other developments:
John Dean pleads guilty to blocking investigation; Howard Hughes loan probed;
bail denied Watergate Seven.

541 October 29, 1973—**Wall Street Journal**.
Believes Richard Nixon's critics hold him at their mercy and very little he can
do to avoid total destruction of his Administration if they fully explore advantages

he has handed them. Hopes that opponents recognize power to destroy a president carries grave responsibilities to the nation and political process.

542   October 30, 1973—**Washington Post**.
       As rebuttal to President's press conference, completely refutes Richard Nixon's version of and reasons for Archibald Cox firing. Quotes some of Nixon's own men, including General Haig, to make points perfectly clear.

543   October 31, 1973—**Discussion**, "Watergate: Religious Issues and Answers,"
       pp. 1080+
       See *Christian Century*, September 26, 1973.

NOVEMBER 1973

544   November 1973—**Esquire**, "Did There Come a Point in Time When There
       Were 43 Different Theories of How Watergate Happened?" Edward J.
       Epstein and John Berendt, pp. 127-32.
       Consolidates briefly all theories proffered thus far, delineating the proponent of the theory, and its selling points and drawbacks, as well as the thesis itself. Theories concern: who masterminded Watergate, what they were after, Richard Nixon was framed, how could it happen, and cover-up.

545   November 1973—**Fortune**, "Watergate as a Case Study in Management," Max
       Ways, pp. 109-11+
       Examines Watergate from a management point of view, poising cost versus effectiveness, poor communication with the Executive, poor target selection. Evaluates Watergate in terms of classic tragedy.

546   November 1973—**Ramparts**, "From Dallas to Watergate: The Longest Cover-
       Up," Peter Dale Scott, pp. 12-20+
       Draws a line from cover-up of John F. Kennedy assassination to Watergate—many of the same people and techniques involved.

547   November 1, 1973—**Los Angeles Times**.
       Says it is asking a great deal to believe that two of most crucial conversations between President Richard Nixon and Watergate principals were not recorded by the elaborate White House bugging apparatus. Two words come to the lips of the nation—incredible and unbelievable.

548   November 1, 1973—**Washington Post**.
       Believes it inconceivable in the strange case of the missing Watergate tapes that the President and his advisers could wait until the last minute before the scheduled delivery of the tapes to Judge Sirica to announce publicly that this vital evidence, in fact, never did exist. Considering previous destruction of evidence, finds it difficult to take at face value this White House assertion.

549   November 2, 1973—**Chicago Tribune**.
Finds Mr. Nixon's appointments of William Saxbe as Attorney General and Leon Jaworski as replacement for Archibald Cox puzzling appointments and not exactly what the American people had in mind.

550   November 2, 1973—**St. Louis Post-Dispatch**.
Questions Leon Jaworski's suitability for special prosecutor since he is friend to John Connally who has been linked to the questionable ITT anti-trust settlement and has possible ties to Texas oil firms accused of illegal contributions to the Nixon campaign.

551   November 2, 1973—**Washington Post**.
Questions Leon Jaworski's independence in prosecution of Watergate cases.

552   November 3, 1973—**America**, "Government of Laws or Men?" p. 319.
Richard Nixon's concession on the tapes seen as political expediency rather than obedience to the law.

553   November 3, 1973—**America**, "Questions and Answers," Edward Glynn, p. 323.
Lists questions arising out of Saturday Night Massacre as to whether President is above the law.

554   November 3, 1973—**New Republic**, "Firing Cox: Gross Miscalculation,"
      Nathan Lewin, pp. 12-13.
Feels Richard Nixon miscalculated in judging Archibald Cox as a Kennedy Democrat and not an impartial lawyer, which he is.

555   November 3, 1973—**New Republic**, "Impeachment and the House," pp. 5-7.
Details work ahead for the House Judiciary Committee: setting up machinery for impeachment, acting on Gerald Ford nomination, and establishing office of Special Prosecutor outside White House control.

556   November 3, 1973—**New Republic**, "Keeping Our Heads: What Now?"
      Alexander M. Bickel, pp. 13-14.
Shows what might have happened had Archibald Cox not been fired and judicial process allowed to continue.

557   November 3, 1973—**New Republic**, "To the Brink," John Osborne, pp. 10-12.
Describes decisions and actions that led to Saturday Night Massacre, and how they contradict statements made by Richard Nixon.

558   November 4, 1973—**Denver Post**.
Declares Watergate situation intolerable and reluctantly comes to the conclusion that if President does not resign only an impeachment proceeding will heal hemorrhaging of national confidence in the presidency.

559   November 4, 1973—**New York Times Magazine**, "Man for This Season," p. 34+
Combination interview-biography of Judge John J. Sirica, with many pro and con comments of his handling of the Watergate case.

560   November 5, 1973—**Newsweek**, "'It Looks Very Grim'," pp. 21-9.
Surveys the backlash to the "Saturday Night Massacre," including serious discussions of impeachment, and first steps taken in that direction. Evaluates Richard Nixon's latest press conference.

561   November 5, 1973—**Newsweek**, "Probe Turns toward Nixon," pp. 29-30.
Areas of Richard Nixon's activities under investigation including real estate deals, tax deductions, pardon and commutations of sentences in return for campaign donations, milk fund, and the Howard Hughes money delineated.

562   November 5, 1973—**Newsweek**, "Watergatology," p. 62.
Foreign reaction to Watergate and particularly Archibald Cox's firing examined.

563   November 5, 1973—**Newsweek**, "What's on Those Nine Tapes?" p. 23.
Speculates as to what might be on the nine subpoenaed tapes according to John Dean's testimony.

564   November 5, 1973—**Time**, "Could the President's Tapes Be Altered?" p. 17.
Enumerates techniques for altering tapes, how alterations can be detected, and how they can be overlooked.

565   November 5, 1973—**Time**, "Seven Tumultuous Days," pp. 13-22.
Chronologizes events of the week following the "Saturday Night Massacre," October 21-27, including public reaction, Richard Nixon's decision to relinquish tapes, biographical sketch of Congressman Peter Rodino, Middle East flare-up, press conference, and search for new special prosecutor.

566   November 5, 1973—**Time**, "Where the Cox Probe Left Off," pp. 23-6.
Mentions areas Archibald Cox was investigating which might have led to his dismissal: Townhouse Project, handling of demonstrators, plumbers, bugging newsmen, the Howard Hughes donation and other illegal campaign contributions.

567   November 5, 1973—**U.S. News**, "After Surrendering Tapes—New Pressures on Nixon," pp. 19-21.
See *Time*, November 5, "Seven Tumultuous Days."

568   November 5, 1973—**U.S. News**, "Elliot Richardson Tells His Side of the Story," pp. 64-5.
Excerpts Elliot Richardson's October 23 press conference, during which he explained his reasons for resigning as Attorney General.

569   November 5, 1973—**U.S. News**, "From the Official Record: Nixon's History-Making Moves," pp. 70-1.
Texts of: Richard Nixon's tapes compromise statement; Archibald Cox's reply; Nixon's letter to acting Attorney General Robert Bork instructing him to fire Cox; and Nixon lawyer Charles Wright's statement acceding to court order for tapes.

570   November 5, 1973–**U.S. News**, "Haig: 'Events That Led to the Fire Storm'," pp. 66-9.
Excerpts General Alexander Haig's news conference of October 23, in which he outlines the administration's reasons for firing Archibald Cox.

571   November 5, 1973–**U.S. News**, "Where the Investigation Started by Archibald Cox Stands Now," p. 20.
See *Time*, November 5, "Where the Cox Probe Left Off."

572   November 6, 1973–**Washington Post**.
Considers calls for President's resignation without impeachment trial a course without formal and final resolution of the allegations against him.

573   November 8, 1973–**Washington Post**.
Comments on presidential charge of lack of perspective in reporting individual Watergate disclosures and suggests that thorough look adds up to present public skepticism concerning Richard Nixon's own good faith and innocence.

574   November 9, 1973–**National Review**, "Stay Tuned," George F. Will, p. 1228.
Satirically repeats background to Saturday Night Massacre.

575   November 9, 1973–**National Review**, "Where Do We Go from Here?" pp. 1220-2.
Calls for Richard Nixon's resignation on basis of accumulation of disbelief in his ability to govern.

576   November 9, 1973–**Newsday**.
Sees consensus emerging that President Richard Nixon's credibility, authority and ability to govern have been damaged irreparably. Calls for approval of Gerald Ford as vice-president at once and beginning of impeachment procedure against Nixon.

577   November 10, 1973–**New Republic**, "Exit Nixon," pp. 5-7.
Repeats recent Richard Nixon statements and shows how they were falsely made: tapes compromise, Howard Hughes donation, and ITT intervention. Calls for Nixon's voluntary resignation, and suggests questions to be put to Gerald Ford before congressional approval is given.

578   November 10, 1973–**New Republic**, "Tales from Tapes," Walter Pincus, pp. 8-9.
Shows how the tapes should either substantiate or refute John Dean's testimony, rather than be interpreted variously as the President suggests.

579   November 10, 1973–**Washington Post**.
In questioning Richard Nixon's credibility, suggests attempt to have seven Watergate tapes made public in efforts to apply a quick fix to public doubts and disbelief, is too little and too late.

580 November 12, 1973—**Newsweek**, "Nixon: What Next?" pp. 24-9.
After Saturday Night Massacre and evidence that Richard Nixon quashed ITT case, now two of subpoenaed tapes missing. Runs down what should be on them. White House explanation for tape lapses presented. Public reaction to this disclosure mentioned.

581 November 12, 1973—**Time**, "Jury of the People Weighs Nixon," pp. 24+
Estimates of various *Time* Bureau Chiefs as to sentiments of their parts of the country on Richard Nixon, Watergate, and impeachment.

582 November 12, 1973—**Time**, "Main Street Revisited: Changing Views on Watergate," p. 29.
Re-interviews of those questioned across the country about Watergate just before the hearings began, to see whether and how their opinions have changed.

583 November 12, 1973—**Time**, "Mystery of the Missing Tapes," pp. 22-23.
See *Newsweek*, November 12.

584 November 12, 1973—**Time**, "Stand-Up Texan for a Tough Task: Leon
Jaworski," pp. 45-6.
Biographical sketch of Leon Jaworski, along with estimates of the job left to do.

585 November 12, 1973—**Time**, "Ultimatum to the President," pp. 38-40.
Lists Republican conditions for continuing to support Richard Nixon after the "Saturday Night Massacre."

586 November 12, 1973—**U.S. News**, "About Those Missing Tapes: White House
Experts' Story," pp. 102-6.
Excerpts court testimony by Fred Buzhardt and Raymond Zumwalt about why two conversations supposed to have been recorded were not.

587 November 12, 1973—**U.S. News**, "Tapes Mystery: Roadblocks Facing New
Prosecutor," pp. 21-3.
Discusses problems facing new prosecutor; latest disclosure that two vital tapes are missing and reactions to it; and difficulties besetting congressional approval of Gerald Ford and William Saxbe.

588 November 12, 1973—**U.S. News**, "What Mitchell and Dean Said about Their
Talks with the President," pp. 104-5.
Excerpts from John Mitchell and John Dean's testimony before the Ervin Committee regarding the conversations that should be on the missing tapes.

589 November 13, 1973—**Washington Post**.
Wonders why Mr. Nixon has chosen this precise time to establish some kind of tribunal of his own and how he can really expect that yielding documents chosen by him can resolve the questions on his fitness to govern.

590   November 14, 1973—**Wall Street Journal**.
      Believes that press coverage of Watergate has been vindicated by events in
spite of friends of the President around the country who insist there has been an
Eastern press cabal, even with such sympathetic criticism as the *Wall Street Journal*
has made.

591   November 16, 1973—**Washington Post**.
      Declares that court-appointed prosecutor would dissipate energy and promote
confusion in task of bringing Watergate offenses to light and Watergate offenders
to justice.

592   November 19, 1973—**Chicago Tribune**.
      Believes Nixon's Florida news conference has not removed all suspicion
against him but has cleared the air, put things in fairer perspective and paved the
way for future appearances, which in time should reduce the credibility gap that
has plagued his Administration.

593   November 19, 1973—**Nation**, "From the Watergate Perspective: Kangaroo
            Grand Juries," Frank J. Donner and Richard I. Lavine, pp. 519-33.
      In-depth examination of the use of grand juries to collect political intelligence,
legitimatizing such evidence, and use of civil contempt to punish.

594   November 19, 1973—**Nation**, "Mound of Skulls," pp. 516-17.
      Reviews trail of dishonored former employees Richard Nixon has left in his
wake, as well as the few who escaped unscathed.

595   November 19, 1973—**Newsweek**, "Luckless Watergate Four," pp. 45-6.
      Resentencing of Watergate Seven described as well as effects the jail terms
have had on the men and their families. Judge Sirica criticized for his handling of
these men.

596   November 19, 1973—**Time**, "How the Public Feels about Nixon and Water-
            gate Now," pp. 25-6.
      Results of public opinion polls on Richard Nixon involvement in Watergate.

597   November 19, 1973—**Time**, "Now a White House Inaudibility Gap," pp. 21-2.
      Discrepancies regarding storing and checking in and out of tapes listed, as
well as first implications that they might be partially inaudible.

598   November 19, 1973—**Time**, "Test for Jaworski," p. 27.
      Indicates potential pitfalls for Leon Jaworski in further investigation. Inti-
mates that if all avenues are not energetically followed, his staff will resign.

599   November 20, 1973—**Philadelphia Inquirer**.
      Finds a welcome change in Richard Nixon going public again after months of
seclusion, and although not answering questions fully, he does talk about Watergate.
Suggests that if he really does want the public to know the truth he can guarantee
the independence of the special prosecutor.

600 November 20, 1973—**St. Louis Post-Dispatch**.
At the end of meeting with newspaper editors in Florida, President Nixon directs television cameras to stay on him so he can "explain" the *quid pro quo* of heavy financial contributions of dairymen. Demonstrates the absurdity of claim that Nixon is victim of networks.

601 November 20, 1973—**Washington Post**.
Disbelieves that President's so-called "Operation Candor" will clear up Watergate and related matters but rather feels that it adds to public confusion. Cites especially his performance before Associated Press managing editors at Disney World.

602 November 21, 1973—**Christian Century**, "Assassination of the Presidency," James M. Wall, pp. 1139-40.
Deplores the fact that young people's opinion of government will come from the Watergate hearings. While a president was assassinated ten years ago, the presidency itself is now suffering the same fate.

603 November 24, 1973—**New Republic**, "Watergate Teasers," Walter Pincus, pp. 14-15.
Answers three questions about tape contents: when did H. R. Haldeman first listen to a tape and what was taped; why will he not admit hearing March 13, 1973 conversation; and how accurate are Secret Service logs on the tapes.

604 November 26, 1973—**Newsweek**, "Mr. Nixon Comes Out Fighting," pp. 24-34.
See *Time*, November 26, "Nixon Presses His Counterattack."

605 November 26, 1973—**Time**, "Nixon Presses His Counterattack," pp. 15-17.
Describes Richard Nixon's activity during the week to assuage public feeling—remarks from a speech made in Florida, meetings with groups of senators and congressmen, and attacking Archibald Cox and Elliot Richardson. Another tape now missing.

606 November 26, 1973—**Time**, "Nothing Is Inviolate," p. 21.
Interview with new Special Prosecutor Leon Jaworski, particularly dealing with subpoenaing of presidential tapes.

607 November 26, 1973—**U.S. News**, "Nixon's All-Out Drive to Restore Confidence," pp. 27-8.
Judge Gesell finds firing of Archibald Cox illegal; Richard Nixon says he will furnish more tapes than required and will meet with lawmakers in small groups to explain his problems.

608 November 26, 1973—**Washington Post**.
Calls missing eighteen minutes from Watergate tape Richard Nixon's Thanksgiving gift and refuses to believe tape was erased by accident.

609   November 28, 1973–**Washington Post**.
With two tapes, one dictabelt and eighteen missing minutes, protests President's claim of executive privilege with regard to part or all of three remaining tapes.

610   November 29, 1973–**Washington Post**.
Says Richard Nixon, by promiscuous use of such terms as "national security," "presidential papers," and "presidential confidentiality," has disqualified himself as a competent judge of what the new special prosecutor's responsibilities are in finding Watergate truth.

DECEMBER 1973

611   Winter 1973–**American Scholar**, "Silent Complicity at Watergate," Howard F. Stein,   pp. 21-37.
In-depth analysis of the social and psychological climate that led to Watergate, and how Richard Nixon and Company fulfilled various American needs.

612   December 1973–**American Bar Association Journal**, "President Nixon: Toughing It Out with the Law," William Van Alstyne, pp. 1398-1402.
Compares Richard Nixon's claim of executive privilege in the tape controversy with his similar positions regarding the G. Harold Carswell nomination, impounding of funds, and domestic wiretapping. Points out that such claims have diverted attention from Nixon's conduct to the question of constitutional power.

613   December 1973–**Association of the Bar of the City of New York City Record**, "Some Reflections on Possible Abuses of Governmental Power," Archibald Cox, pp. 811-27.
Calls for return to concepts of right and wrong rather than mere political expediency. Discusses the areas and scope of the Special Prosecutor's investigations and how his effectiveness should be measured.

614   December 1973–**Current**, "Toward Resignation or Impeachment?" pp. 3-6.
See *National Review*, November 9, "Where Do We Go from Here?"

615   December 1973–**Discussion**, "Appointment with Watergate," Seymour Martin Lipset and Earl Raab, pp. 4+
See *Commentary*, September 1973.

616   December 1973–**International Socialist Review**, "Left and Watergate," Cliff Conner, pp. 12-17+
Explains socialists' anti-Richard Nixon efforts since Watergate, including lawsuits and impeachment efforts. Chinese and Russian reactions to Watergate spelled out.

617   December 1973–**International Socialist Review**, "Watergate and the White House: From Kennedy to Nixon and Beyond," Les Evans, pp. 4-11+
Examines Richard Nixon's background and unrest in the country that formed the basis for Watergate. Development of "counter-insurgency" traced.

618   December 2, 1973—**Washington Post.**
Believes that in spite of presidential roadblocks and efforts to hamstring Leon Jaworski that the Special Prosecutor is moving ahead vigorously and effectively on all fronts.

619   December 3, 1973—**Newsweek,** "Answers That Raise Fresh Questions," p. 27.
Compares recent "Operation Candor" statements with previous ones by President Richard Nixon, highlighting discrepancies between them.

620   December 3, 1973—**Newsweek,** "New Tale of the Tapes," pp. 26-33.
Describes Operation Candor and the 18 minute tape buzz that again destroys Richard Nixon's credibility.

621   December 3, 1973—**Time,** "Round 2 in Nixon's Counterattack," pp. 15-17.
Recounts latest Watergate bombshell—18 minute buzz obliterates important section of a tape. Rose Mary Woods explanation refuted by the tape experts. Tells of continued White House attempts to discredit Elliot Richardson.

622   December 3, 1973—**Time,** "Staff Cox Left Behind," pp. 18-21.
Describes Special Prosecutor's task forces and their leaders' backgrounds.

623   December 3, 1973—**U.S. News,** "Watergate's Impact on Future as Political Scientists See It," pp. 78-82.
Results of a poll among political scientists about the impact of Watergate on the voting public, future elections, and possible changes in the political system.

624   December 8, 1973—**America,** "Time Not To Be Away," Mary McGrory, p. 437.
Expresses author's chagrin at being out of the country during the Saturday Night Massacre. Finds it hard to understand why the nation finally reacted to that. Comments Operation Candor seems chiefly to be destroying Elliot Richardson's reputation.

625   December 8, 1973—**Chicago Tribune.**
Questions the appointment of Senator William Saxbe as Attorney General because of constitutional prohibitions against congressional appointment to a federal job where pay has been raised during current term in Congress.

626   December 8, 1973—**New Republic,** "At the Death," John Osborne, pp. 8-10.
The official White House story about loss of two tapes and partial erasure of another given, then contrasted with previous statements of those involved.

627   December 8, 1973—**New Republic,** "Cox Investigation," Walter Pincus, pp. 10-13.
Details the aspects of the Archibald Cox investigation that are now being taken up by Leon Jaworski: Watergate burglary, illegal campaign funding, dirty tricks, wiretapping, potential criminal offenses involving governmental abuses of power, and ITT.

628 December 10, 1973—**Newsweek**, "Doing the Twist While Erasing the Tape,"
    p. 28.
Records opinion of experts about whether Miss Rose Mary Woods' story of
the tape could be true.

629 December 10, 1973—**Newsweek**, "Rose Mary's Boo-Boo," pp. 26-32.
Lists most recent difficulties with Watergate—trials and indictments, dis-
satisfaction with Leon Jaworski and Fred Buzhardt. Deals primarily with Rose
Mary Woods' 18 minute tape hum—how she claims it happened, what might have
been on tape, and why it was not disclosed before.

630 December 10, 1973—**Time**, "Fuse Burns Ever Closer," p. 24.
Egil Krogh pleads guilty in Ellsberg burglary and will tell all he knows about
plumbers' activities. Dwight Chapin indicted.

631 December 10, 1973—**Time**, "Lost Momentum and Broken Unity," p. 26.
Explains why Ervin Committee is suspending hearings until January: investigations not complete, White House and Howard Hughes refusing to comply with
subpoenas, and Senator Gurney being investigated.

632 December 10, 1973—**Time**, "Secretary and the Tapes Tangle," pp. 15-22.
Repeats history of tapes controversy and the Rose Mary Woods tape erasure.
Detailed description of her testimony and demonstration of how it happened.
Much biographical material of Miss Woods provided. Explains how technical panel
will test the tape.

633 December 10, 1973—**U.S. News**, "One More Surprise in the Watergate Case,"
    pp. 35-6.
Repeats revelation of and Rose Mary Woods' testimony regarding 18 minute
tape buzz. Dwight Chapin is indicted, while Egil Krogh pleads guilty in Ellsberg
burglary.

634 December 10, 1973—**U.S. News**, "Watergate Prosecutor Charts the Next
    Moves," pp. 37-8.
Interview with Leon Jaworski about: his independence, areas of investigation,
staff, and plumbers.

635 December 11, 1973—**Chicago Tribune**.
Says Mr. Nixon should be treated like other taxpayers after his disclosure of
finances and tax returns. His worst proved offense has been poor judgment and as
for tax liability and talk of impeachment, critics will have to be more specific than
they have been so far.

636 December 11, 1973—**Los Angeles Times**.
Takes Mr. Nixon to task for not paying his fair share of income taxes.

637 December 11, 1973—**New York Times**.
In discussing what appears to be full disclosure of Richard Nixon financial
affairs, makes the point that our tax system depends on cooperation of millions of

private citizens which cannot survive if shown that those who set examples are instead taking advantage of loopholes and walking narrow line between legal and illegal.

638 December 12, 1973—**St. Louis Post-Dispatch.**
Believes Richard Nixon financial data was not made public in gesture of candor but was issued in desperate attempt to stem mounting pressure for impeachment or resignation. Compares leniency in resolving his tax evasion to that of average citizen.

639 December 12, 1973—**Wall Street Journal**, "Issues beyond Watergate," Philip B. Kurland, p. 20.
Feels who did what relatively unimportant. The relevant questions are how did we arrive at this stage and what is the solution to it? Corruption of the Constitution is the problem. Suggests the White House as fourth branch of government should be eliminated.

640 December 14, 1973—**Science**, "Watergate: Verification of Tapes May Be Electronic Standoff," Nicholas Wade, pp. 1108-10.
In-depth examination of how presidential tapes can be analyzed by Judge Sirica's panel for tampering.

641 December 17, 1973—**Nation**, "'What, in Our House?'" Carl Cohen and Robert Green, p. 657.
Contends when truth is involved, a natural response will come; if not, the response will be inappropriate. Illustrates with Richard Nixon responses to questions about missing tapes.

642 December 17, 1973—**Newsweek**, "'As if We've Turned Some Kind of Corner'," pp. 24-8.
Shows how, as Gerald Ford is sworn in as Vice President, Richard Nixon's power continues to erode. Rose Mary Woods sticks to her story, but more holes in it pointed up now.

643 December 17, 1973—**Time**, "Another Week of Strain," pp. 17-18.
Covers testimony of Rose Mary Woods, General Alexander Haig, and Lawrence Higby on the tape erasure. New developments regarding Howard Hughes money and milk fund mentioned.

644 December 17, 1973—**Time**, "God and Watergate," p. 78.
Questions frequent failure of the clergy to comment on or condemn Watergate. Lists those who have taken a stance, as well as notable recent silences.

645 December 17, 1973—**U.S. News**, "Vice President Ford: 'Why I Will Not Run in '76'," pp. 24-30.
Interview with Gerald Ford covers future political ambitions, handling of Watergate by present Administration, possible impeachment, Watergate's effect on future elections, and his ideas on government policies.

646 December 17, 1973—**U.S. News**, "Watergate Tapes—The Puzzle Persists,"
     p. 37.
     Goes over the testimony concerning the 18 minute tape erasure.

647 December 21, 1973—**National Review**, "Canto 476: Rose Mary Woods,"
     pp. 1394-6.
     Shows how Miss Rose Mary Woods' story of the 18 minute tape erasure lacks
credibility when considered with overall handling of the tapes.

648 December 21, 1973—**National Review**, "Goal Line Stand," p. 1400.
     Compares Richard Nixon's successful first term counterattack of "sub-
versives" with failing "Operation Candor," pretty well done to death by Rose Mary
Woods' tape caper.

649 December 22, 1973—**New Republic**, "Prosecutor Jaworski's Operation Town-
     house," Walter Pincus, pp. 10-11.
     Outlines the details of the Republican "Townhouse" plan to collect and dis-
burse secret contributions to candidates to unseat Democratic incumbents.

650 December 24, 1973—**Newsweek**, "Watergate: Drip, Drip, Drip," pp. 17-18.
     Relates evidence of panel of tape experts that finds Miss Rose Mary Woods'
story highly unlikely. Richard Nixon's disclosure of his taxes boomerangs, especially regarding deductions for his Vice-Presidential papers.

651 December 24, 1973—**Time**, "Holiday Test for the President," pp. 9-10.
     Repeats experts' report on lack of feasibility of Rose Mary Woods' tape buzz
story. Several unsubpoenaed tapes volunteered by Richard Nixon.

652 December 29, 1973—**New Republic**, "CIA and the Plumbers," Tad Szulc,
     pp. 19-21.
     Delineates new information on CIA involvement at behest of White House
before and during plumbers: support of President Kaunda's government in Zambia;
burglary at ITT; investigation of Daniel Ellsberg by British Embassy employees; and
supplying of equipment to plumbers.

653 December 31, 1973—**Newsweek**, "Watergate's Legacy for '74," pp. 10-11.
     Mentions new tape subpoenas; Richard Nixon may fight on basis of executive
privilege and recent leaks. Politicians' thoughts on impeachment repeated, as well
as new Nixon problems regarding tax deductions.

654 December 31, 1973—**Time**, "President Yields to Congress," pp. 10-11.
     Judge Sirica screening tapes, finds several not applicable. Playing of one of
tapes by lawyer William Dubrovir at party condemned by White House. Mentions
hiring of John Doar as special counsel to House Judiciary Committee.

BOOKS

655 **All the President's Men.** Carl Bernstein and Bob Woodward. New York, Simon
and Schuster, 1974. 349p. $8.95.
Written by the two investigative reporters from the *Washington Post* who
were responsible for breaking the Watergate story, this book traces their search for
information on the burglary and cover-up. Photos. Index.

656 **American Life: One Man's Road to Watergate.** Jeb Stuart Magruder. New
York, Atheneum, 1974. 370p. $10.00.
In the first two chapters, Jeb Magruder describes his early days and business
career, but the rest of the book is dedicated to his White House days, with much
detail on Watergate and the cover-up. Index.

657 **Compulsive Spy: The Strange Career of E. Howard Hunt.** Tad Szulc. New
York, Viking, 1974. 180p. $5.95.
This book details the career of E. Howard Hunt from his OSS days in Burma,
to his CIA work in Europe and Latin America. It culminates with his activities pre-,
during, and post-Watergate.

658 **Mask of State: Watergate Portraits.** Mary McCarthy. New York, Harcourt,
1974. 165p. $6.95.
Ms. McCarthy has revised and enlarged six articles written for the London
Observer and two for the *New York Review of Books* dated from June 17, 1973,
to March 7, 1974. The primary accent is on the progress of the hearings and
characters of the participants. No index.

659 **Presidential Transcripts.** *Washington Post* Staff. New York, Dell, 1974. 693p.
$2.45.
One of a number of publications of the tape transcripts available in paperback.
Also available in hardback from the Government Printing Office.

660 **Senate Watergate Report.** Senate Select Committee on Presidential Campaign
Activities. New York, Dell, 1974. 2 vols. $2.75 each.
Presents the complete final report of the Ervin Committee in paperback form.

661 **They Could Not Trust the King.** Stanley Tretick. New York, Collier, 1974.
197p. $4.95.
Primarily a non-chronological photographic essay on Watergate, with connec-
tive, explanatory notes.

662 **Watergate and the White House July-December 1973.** Vol. 2. Edward
Knappman. New York, Facts on File, 1974. 290p. $4.75.
Part 1 covers the Watergate events beginning with John Mitchell's testimony
and ending with confirmation of William Saxbe as Attorney General. Part 2
reproduces editorials from 120 major U.S. newspapers on each of the key events.
Contains biographical sketches of those involved. Chronology of events on inside
covers. Index.

663 **Watergate and the White House, January-September 1974.** Vol. 3. Edward
  Knappman. New York, Facts on File, 1974. 416p. $5.25.
  The final volume in the Watergate series, this one is arranged chronologically,
carrying the events through the pardoning of Richard Nixon. Part 2 contains important editorials. Once again a biographical section is included along with a brief
chronology in the inner covers. Index.

664 **Watergate: Chronology of a Crisis.** Vol. 2. Washington, D.C., Congressional
  Quarterly, 1974. 432p. $7.50.
  Reprints all articles from the *Weekly Reports* from August 25,1973, to May 4,
1974. Following each week's entries is an annotated chronology of the week's
events. Includes profiles of those involved, in-depth analysis of events, and textual
reprints of many appropriate statements, letters, memos, and transcripts. Indexed.

JANUARY 1974

665 Vol. 20, No. 1, 1974—**Loyola Law Review**, "Controlling 'Executive Privilege'," Sam J. Ervin, Jr. pp. 11-31.
  Illustrates how executive privilege was created by the Executive Branch, not
by the Constitution or statute. Excerpts Senator Muskie-Attorney General Richard
Kleindienst exchanges on the subject at 1973 hearings and Muskie-Elliot Richardson
discussion the same year. Examines provisions of proposed S.2432 bill on executive
privilege.

666 Vol. 20, No. 1, 1974—**Loyola Law Review**, "Executive Privilege . . . Growth
  of Power over a Declining Congress," Luis Kutner, pp. 33-44.
  In-depth discussion of concept and uses of executive privilege. Traces its use
by various administrations, culminating in Watergate-related invocation of it by
President Richard Nixon.

667 Vol. 20, No. 1, 1974—**Loyola Law Review**, "Historic Confrontation between
  Government and Press," Turner Catledge, pp. 1-10.
  Explores the relationship of various presidents with the press, culminating
in anti-Richard Nixon era and press investigation into Watergate. Accents importance of free press in keeping the government honest.

668 Vol. 35, No. 1, 1974—**Ohio State Law Journal**, "Executive Privilege, the Congress and the Courts," Norman Dorsen and John H. F. Shattuck, pp. 1-40.
  Expresses reasons for the authors' belief that the assertion of discretionary
executive privilege by Richard Nixon in White House tapes issue is without basis in
historical or judicial precedent and discusses the extent to which a president may
claim confidentiality.

669 January 1974—**American Bar Association Journal**, "What Really Happened to
  the Jefferson Subpoenas," Irwin S. Rhodes, pp. 52-4.
  Suggests that the arguments and issues of the Watergate Tapes Case are similar
to those of the Aaron Burr trial and that those who opposed, in the former, the
absolute character of executive privilege, departed from precedent set by Chief
Justice Marshall.

670 January 1974—**Atlantic**, "Undoing of the Justice Department: After the 'Saturday Night Massacre'," Sanford J. Ungar, pp. 29-34.
Describes the history of the Department of Justice during the Nixon Administration. Shows how the department took a political turn it hadn't had since Robert F. Kennedy, culminating in the Saturday Night Massacre.

671 January 1974—**Commentary**, "Watergate and the Legal Order," Alexander M. Bickel, pp. 19-25.
Suggests that the Watergate affair was inevitable because the Vietnam War and preceding conditions, affecting the nation's legal and social order, constituted a prologue to it.

672 January 1974—**Ramparts**, "Behind the Scenes at the Cox Investigation," George Lardner, Jr., pp. 21-6.
Summarizes Archibald Cox's hiring, political background, conduct of the investigation, his staffers' backgrounds, and his firing.

673 January-February 1974—**California Bar Journal**, "'Each Branch Shall Be Independent': The Burr-Watergate Syndrome," Everett B. Clary, pp. 17-23+
Presents historic background of John Marshall-Thomas Jefferson confrontation in the Aaron Burr case. Its similarities to the Watergate case enumerated.

674 January-February 1974—**Case and Comment**, "Executive Privilege: The Need for Congressional Action," Sam J. Ervin, Jr., pp. 39-48.
Reviews the varying positions of Nixon on the exercise of executive privilege, including that which he took on the Watergate tapes. Demonstrates the difficulty of defining the privilege and states the author's interpretation of it.

675 January-February 1974—**Today's Education**, "Watergate and the Classroom," Hugh Sidey, pp. 23-5.
Mentions various courses set up across the nation to study aspects of Watergate. Lists what he feels are necessary steps to rid us all of the Watergate mentality.

676 January 5, 1974—**New Republic**, "Babble on the Tapes," Walter Pincus, pp. 11-13.
Examines conflicts in tapes testimony: where was Secret Service when tape ran out; what happened to nine tapes during Rose Mary Woods' typing; why was 18 minute buzz not disclosed earlier.

677 January 5, 1974—**Washington Post**.
Doesn't wish to see a bruising constitutional battle between branches of government but sees Richard Nixon's refusal to honor Watergate Committee subpoenas as one that must be fought to test the elasticism of our basic charter.

678 January 7, 1974—**Time**, "Cutting Back on Candor," p. 23.
Describes playing of tape at a party by lawyer William Dubrovir and subsequent White House desire to submit transcripts instead of tapes.

679   January 7, 1974—**Time**, "Judge John J. Sirica: Standing Firm for the Primacy of Law," pp. 8-20.
Goes over the events of the year both in Watergate and internationally, focusing on Judge Sirica's actions.

680   January 10, 1974—**Chicago Tribune**.
Mentions President Nixon's defense of his actions in the milk and ITT cases. Calls for more communicative attitude on the part of the White House.

681   January 11, 1974—**Washington Post**.
Comments on discrepancies between President Nixon's statements regarding ITT and other facts. Condemns him for his failure to see impropriety in his actions.

682   January 13, 1974—**New York Times Magazine**, "Cox and His Army," pp. 32-4+
Describes Archibald Cox's personality and background, his actions and resultant White House irritation, and five task forces' areas of exploration.

683   January 13, 1974—**New York Times Magazine**, "Story Continued," J. Anthony Lukas, pp. 2+
Gives background to revelation of presidential tapes' existence and resultant subpoenas.

684   January 13, 1974—**Newsday**.
Calls for speeding up impeachment process, since the country is already suffering from the supposed effects of impeachment disunity already.

685   January 14, 1974—**Newsweek**, "Back on the Counterattack," pp. 18-19.
Outlines recent events: Richard Nixon refuses to honor Ervin Committee subpoena for 600 tapes; Bernard Barker and E. Howard Hunt released from jail; IRS checking into Nixon's taxes; report on tape hum due; and James St. Clair hired as new Nixon lawyer.

686   January 14, 1974—**Time**, "No Respite in the Western White House," p. 9.
Lists latest Richard Nixon problems: IRS investigation, refusal to comply with latest subpoenas, and hiring of James St. Clair for his attorney.

687   January 16, 1974—**Washington Post**.
Comments on destruction of evidence in erasure of White House tape and states another event has demonstrated the worthlessness of White House testimony in a federal court on a criminal matter.

688   January 17, 1974—**Washington Post**.
In response to Vice President Gerald Ford's challenge for would-be impeachers to quit dragging their feet and resolve Richard Nixon's innocence or guilt, the *Post* enumerates the instances of White House artful dodging against those who would get to bottom of Watergate.

689   January 18, 1974–**National Review**, "British View of Watergate," Ferdinand
          Mount, p. 77+
      Feels ethical standards are now unenforceable and unrealistic and tend to
make ordinary men look suspicious. Laws only deal with effects, not causes, as
they should.

690   January 18, 1974–**National Review**, "White House Tapes: Continued," p. 70+
      Notes announcement that tapes will not be made public. Feels it is due to
fact that they may be easily "misinterpreted" regarding Richard Nixon's
involvement.

691   January 19, 1974–**New Republic**, "Those Missing 18 Minutes," George
          O'Toole, pp. 15-18.
      Former CIA official explains how the missing 18 minutes might be recovered
by tape experts.

692   January 20, 1974–**Washington Post**.
      Says impasse in Watergate affairs caused by President's setting up roadblocks
against both processes by which he might be held accountable for misconduct in
office is intolerable.

693   January 21, 1974–**Newsweek**, "I'd Wondered What Became of Sally," Shana
          Alexander, p. 32.
      Satiric discussion of secretarial virtues of Sally Harmony and Richard Nixon's
Operation Candor white papers as instead being tattletale gray.

694   January 21, 1974–**Newsweek**, "Stepping Up the Pressure," pp. 19-20.
      Special Prosecutor Leon Jaworski implies he will ask for more tapes and that
the President may be indictable while in office and called as witness in trials.
Offers Richard Nixon's latest assertions about milk fund and ITT. Other problems:
Sally Harmony states she filled in $50,000 in blank checks from Howard Hughes,
and IRS finds tax returns incorrect.

695   January 21, 1974–**Time**, "Awaiting the Next Round in Watergate," pp. 11-12.
      Latest Watergate developments: John Ehrlichman meets with Leon Jaworski
but no deal made; experts to submit report on tape buzz; plumbers discovered
Pentagon to be spying on Henry Kissinger. Mentions end of Operation Candor and
release of two papers by Richard Nixon on milk and ITT cases.

696   January 24, 1974–**New York Times**.
      Calls Vice President Ford and Senator Scott to task for unsupported state-
ments regarding Nixon's innocence. Refers to them as the latest victims of Nixon's
games.

697   January 26, 1974–**America**, "Of Many Things," Donald R. Campion, inside
          cover.
      Reflects that public seems to be losing interest in Watergate, perhaps because
of more immediate economic concerns or general downgrading in power of the
presidency.

698   January 28, 1974–**Newsweek**, "How the Tape Sleuths Did It," p. 17.
      Describes how the panel of tape experts examined the erased tape and came
to their conclusions.

699   January 28, 1974–**Newsweek**, "Probing the Telltale Tape," pp. 14-20.
      Details panel's findings about multiple erasures causing 18 minute tape lapse
and how this invalidates previous explanations. Speculates as to when and how and
by whom it was done.

700   January 28, 1974–**Time**, "Sherlock Holmes: The Case of the Strange Era-
      sures," Stefan Kanfer, pp. 28-9.
      Satire of 18 minute tape erasure as it might have been solved by Sherlock
Holmes.

701   January 28, 1974–**Time**, "Telltale Tape Deepens Nixon's Dilemma,"
      pp. 13-18.
      Reports in detail how tape experts assert 18 minute gap resulted from five to
nine deliberate erasures. Points up failure of Operation Candor. Depicts subsequent
testimony of various White House people regarding handling of the tapes and discrepancies in Rose Mary Woods' various statements.

702   January 28, 1974–**U.S. News**, "Mystery Deepens on Watergate Tapes,"
      pp. 22-3.
      Repeats findings of tape experts on the 18 minute erasure and records various
public reactions to it.

703   January 29, 1974–**Washington Post**.
      Suggests a full explication of Watergate tangle by Senate Watergate Committee
may be too much to ask but wants more compact and careful public hearings to dispel some of the mystery of the strange and secret ways in which so much money,
power and influence have operated en route to the 1972 elections.

FEBRUARY 1974

704   February 1974–**American Bar Association Journal**, "Presidency and Separa-
      tion of Power," Ben R. Miller, pp. 195-7.
      Claims Richard Nixon's refusal to turn over materials subpoenaed by Special
Prosecutor Archibald Cox was based on sound constitutional principles of separation of powers and precedents set by former presidents. Supports Nixon's right to
fire Cox.

705   February 1974–**Harvard Journal on Legislation**, "Congress versus the Execu-
      tive: The Role of the Courts," Raul R. Tapia, John P. James, and Richard
      O. Levine, pp. 352-403.
      Analyzes recent cases in which Congress has gone to court over executive
resistance to requests for information and discusses possible reasons for the increasing occurrence of such suits.

706 February 2, 1974—**New Republic**, "Who Dunnit?" Walter Pincus, pp. 14-17.
Examines discrepancies between Rosé Mary Woods' first description of the erased tapes and presence of H. R. Haldeman, and her later descriptions and exclusion of Haldeman, how and when the tape was erased, and when and where the President was informed about it.

707 February 3, 1974—**Chicago Tribune**.
Feels detailed definition of "high crimes and misdemeanors" is undesirable because such definitions should be able to change in future with the times and public opinion.

708 February 3, 1974—**Los Angeles Times**.
Suggests vote on articles of impeachment not be taken until all the information is in.

709 February 4, 1974—**Newsweek**, "Ervin Calls Off the Show," p. 19.
Examines proposed areas of final hearings by Ervin Committee on milk fund and Bebe Rebozo's fund-raising activities. Lists questions involved in these areas and reasons for postponing hearings "temporarily."

710 February 4, 1974—**Time**, "Nixon Digs In to Fight," pp. 13-14.
Reiterates Richard Nixon's latest attempts to fight out Watergate, including Senator Hugh Scott's contention that John Dean perjured. Ervin Committee votes to examine Howard Hughes money and milk fund. While Egil Krogh clears Nixon of plumbers' burglary involvement, his income tax problems solidify.

711 February 4, 1974—**U.S. News**, "If Nixon Is Impeached—What Then?" pp. 22-9.
Presents an interview with Attorney General William Saxbe on mechanics of impeachment, various presidential tapes aspects, present status of Justice Department, plea bargaining, oil and antitrust laws, and integration.

712 February 11, 1974—**Time**, "Animals in the Forest," p. 26.
Reports latest tape exposure: CIA tapes of conversations with plumbers destroyed in January 1973, one day after request by Mike Mansfield to safeguard any pertinent information. Explains how Senator Howard Baker discovered their existence and requested them.

713 February 11, 1974—**Time**, "Drive to Discredit Dean," pp. 12-14.
Outlines latest attempts to discredit John Dean's Senate testimony by release of some tape transcripts. Explains how import of his testimony is being misunderstood and his veracity upheld.

714 February 11, 1974—**Time**, "Subpoena for Nixon," p. 14.
Examines alternatives facing President Richard Nixon in answering the subpoena for his appearance in the Ellsberg burglary trial of John Ehrlichman, David Young, and G. Gordon Liddy.

715   February 11, 1974—**Time**, "What Price Watergate?" p. 13.
Enumerates costs incurred thus far in the various Watergate investigations to the government and to those under indictment.

716   February 11, 1974—**U.S. News**, "Watergate: More Pressure on President,"
        p. 24.
Examines new issue—can the President be compelled to testify in a criminal trial? Question raised by request for his testimony by John Ehrlichman, Gordon Liddy, and David Young in Ellsberg burglary trial. Includes latest Richard Nixon statements indicating he may refuse to supply further tapes to Leon Jaworski and impeachment committee.

717   February 15, 1974—**National Review**, "Whew!" George F. Will, p. 190.
Satirically states how wonderful that Senator Scott can assure us of John Dean's perjury on the basis of White House-prepared transcripts. Shows that country is concerned about Watergate.

718   February 16, 1974—**Nation**, "Real Impasse," p. 197.
Presents Elliot Richardson's suggestions about how to overcome the impasse of whether it is legal to turn grand jury materials over to the Judiciary Committee.

719   February 16, 1974—**New Republic**, "Cornered," John Osborne, pp. 14-15.
Discusses why Senator Hugh Scott announced transcripts he had read showed John Dean to be lying; more tapes requested by Leon Jaworski likely to be refused and investigation abandoned. Jaworski has publicly indicated his intention to search not only for indictable but also impeachable offenses.

720   February 17, 1974—**St. Louis Post-Dispatch**.
Holds Richard M. Nixon's latest refusal to supply tapes and documents shows his defense has disintegrated into obstructionism.

721   February 18, 1974—**Newsweek**, "Psywar on the Potomac," pp. 25-7.
Recaps Richard Nixon's refusal to submit further tapes to Leon Jaworski and possibility of further defections with indictments upcoming. General Haig's attempts to back up Senator Scott's assertions of John Dean's perjury mentioned.

722   February 18, 1974—**Time**, "Jaworski: Seeing It Through," pp. 10-11.
Presents an interview with Leon Jaworski dealing with obtaining further evidence.

723   February 18, 1974—**Time**, "Pointed Questions for the President," p. 12.
Repeats questions sent by Senator Lowell Weicker to President Richard Nixon in lieu of President's appearance before the Ervin Committee and the basis for these questions.

724   February 18, 1974—**U.S News**, "High Toll of Watergate: 29 Accused, 21
        Found Guilty, More Trials Ahead," pp. 28-9.
Enumerates those thus far indicted and tried in various Watergate cases.

725   February 18, 1974–**U.S. News**, "Impeachment: Congress Puts Nixon under a
       Microscope," pp. 27-9.
       Lists steps taken to set up the impeachment committee and their areas of
inquiry, as well as current status of Ervin Committee inquiry and Leon Jaworski's
attempts to secure more tapes.

726   February 20, 1974–**Chicago Tribune**.
       Feels loss of Gerald Ford's congressional seat is no indication of significant
migration of Republicans to the Democratic party.

727   February 22, 1974–**Science**, "Watergate Tapes: Critics Question Main Conclu-
       sion of Expert Panel," Nicholas Wade, pp. 732-4.
       Presents an alternative to deliberate tape erasure finding of the panel: a defec-
tive circuit in the recorder could have caused it. Repeats portions of court testimony
indicating failure of panel to check out this theory.

728   February 23, 1974–**New Republic**, "Why the Tapes Are Needed," pp. 7-9.
       Contends the number of tapes submitted to the Special Prosecutor should not
be limited. Suggests some tapes that could prove enlightening about executive clemency, and attempts to use CIA in cover-up.

729   February 25, 1974–**Newsweek**, "No, No, A Thousand Times, No!" pp. 26-7.
       Outlines Richard Nixon's refusal to release more tapes, reasons for refusing,
and reaction by Judiciary Committee. Mentions possibility of two tapes being
copies, not originals.

730   February 25, 1974–**Time**, "Quiet-Stall Survival Strategy," pp. 12-13.
       Mentions upcoming indictments and Special Prosecutor Leon Jaworski's
difficulties in obtaining more tapes.

731   February 25, 1974–**U.S. News**, "Now a Rebuff to Jaworski–More Legal Con-
       flict?" p. 23.
       Special Prosecutor Leon Jaworski denied access to more tapes, but no similar
denial thus far to impeachment committee. Mentions possible steps both might
take to acquire them.

732   February 25, 1974–**Wall Street Journal**.
       Discusses pros and cons of basing articles of impeachment on criminal
offenses and decides that is the most practical approach.

MARCH 1974

733   Spring 1974–**American Scholar**, "Public Morality: Afterthoughts on Water-
       gate," Vermont Royster, pp. 249-59.
       Compares Spiro Agnew and Watergaters in that both engaged in activities that
have occurred and been viewed with public apathy in the past. Asserts Watergate
happened because men confused means and ends, which is true of many of us today.

734   Spring 1974—**Yale Review**, "Some Notes on Watergate and America,"
        William Lee Miller, pp. 321-3.
Author's thoughts on vast materials Watergate has supplied for both political
humorists and political moralists.

735   March 1974—**Progressive**, "Selling the People Short," pp. 5-6.
Claims the public desires action in Watergate—cites recent polls. Feels politicians ignoring this for their own political ends.

736   March 2, 1974—**Nation**, "Playing Games," p. 258.
Replays the latest Richard Nixon "games" regarding "cooperation" with
Special Prosecutor's office and Senator Scott's announcement of John Dean's
"perjury."

737   March 2, 1974—**New Republic**, "More on the Tapes," pp. 7-10.
Lists five tapes which might shed further light on hush money, Richard
Nixon's knowledge of cover-up, and the Nixon/H. R. Haldeman discussion of tape
contents.

738   March 4, 1974—**New Yorker**, "Letter from Washington," Richard H. Rovere,
        pp. 90-4.
Examines Cold War history that led to Watergate, and foreign reaction to our
handling of it.

739   March 4, 1974—**Newsweek**, "Vote of No Confidence," pp. 16-19.
Recaps many problems facing President Richard Nixon: loss of Gerald Ford's
seat, upcoming indictments including Jake Jacobsen's, and tax investigation.

740   March 9, 1974—**New Republic**, "Rose Mary's Machine and the 18 Minute
        Gap," George O'Toole, pp. 10-12.
Discusses the Dektor theory of the 18 minute tape gap, then lists several
unanswerable questions still remaining if this explanation is accepted.

741   March 9, 1974—**Saturday Review/World**, "Reflections on a Firestorm,"
        Archibald Cox, pp. 12-14+
Suggests various ways to restore the public's sense of moral limits in politics,
including the impeachment process and reforms in campaign financing.

742   March 10, 1974—**New York Times Magazine**, "Throwing the Book at Him,"
        Russell Baker, p. 6.
Satirical fantasy on sentencing for Watergaters not being the same as for non-
white collar convicts.

743   March 11, 1974—**New Yorker**, "Reporter in Washington, D.C.: Autumn
        Notes-1," Elizabeth Drew, pp. 42-101.
Day-to-day coverage of Watergate and other Washington events from September 5, 1973, to October 25, 1973.

744 March 11, 1974–**Newsweek**, "Jury Points a Finger at Nixon," pp. 17-22.
Details grand jury indictments against Robert Mardian, John Mitchell, John Ehrlichman, H. R. Haldeman, Gordon Strachan, Charles Colson, and Kenneth Parkinson. Inset lists current legal status of 23 Watergaters.

745 March 11, 1974–**Newsweek**, "'Real Softspoken S.O.B.','" p. 30.
Mentions the current conduct of Leon Jaworski and his prosecution team, with brief biographical sketch of Jaworski.

746 March 11, 1974–**Newsweek**, "Story of the Big Cover-Up," pp. 23-9.
Close examination of grand jury indictments of John Mitchell, H. R. Haldeman, John Ehrlichman, Charles Colson, Gordon Strachan, Robert Mardian, and Kenneth Parkinson on cover-up charges and detailed account of the cover-up.

747 March 11, 1974–**Time**, "Other Nixon Watergate Men," pp. 20-1.
Lists 18 Nixon men indicted, convicted, or who pleaded guilty to various charges.

748 March 11, 1974–**Time**, "Seven Charged, a Report and a Briefcase," pp. 11-27.
In-depth report on the Watergate grand jury findings including: list of people indicted and charges; progress of cover-up; possible defense strategies; and Herbert Kalmbach's illegal activities.

749 March 11, 1974–**Time**, "Texan Who Goes His Own Way," pp. 12-13.
See *Newsweek*, March 11, 1974, "Real Softspoken S.O.B."

750 March 11, 1974–**U.S. News**, "Charges against White House," pp. 21-4.
Details grand jury indictments and facts upon which they were based, as well as listing all previous indictments and sentences in Watergate.

751 March 14, 1974–**Los Angeles Times**.
Calls for Nixon's cooperation with the Judiciary Committee.

752 March 14, 1974–**Wall Street Journal**.
Feels the Judiciary Committee should take their time exploring the evidence and not hastily vote for impeachment on the basis of Nixon's refusal to supply the tapes.

753 March 15, 1974–**National Review**, "Scope of the Disaster," p. 298.
Lists current legal statuses of: Herbert Kalmbach, John Mitchell, Maurice Stans, John Ehrlichman, Egil Krogh, David Young, Gordon Liddy, Fred LaRue, Dwight Chapin, Donald Segretti, John Dean, Jeb Magruder, Herbert Porter, and Jake Jacobsen.

754 March 16, 1974–**Nation**, "Continuing Conspiracy," p. 322.
Lauds grand jury for their logical listing of the indictments. Points to indications of presidential involvement hinted at by grand jury's behavior.

755   March 16, 1974—**New Republic**, "Indictments," John Osborne, pp. 11-13.
      Discusses grand jury indictments of Richard Nixon aides and what they may show about his own involvement. Notes President's supposed reaction to the indictments.

756   March 16, 1974—**New Republic**, "That Bulging Briefcase," Nathan Lewin, pp. 13-16.
      Investigates what might have happened had the President been indicted by the Watergate grand jury.

757   March 18, 1974—**New Yorker**, "Reporter in Washington, D.C.: Autumn Notes-II," Elizabeth Drew, pp. 41-105.
      Continues Ms. Drew's reports of Washington and Watergate happenings from October 28, 1973-December 21, 1973.

758   March 18, 1974—**Newsweek**, "'Bag Job', at Dr. Fielding's," pp. 31-9.
      In-depth examination of events leading to the Ellsberg burglary, with the accent on the White House-directed plumbers' activities.

759   March 18, 1974—**Newsweek**, "'I Know What I Meant'," pp. 22-6.
      Recounts President Richard Nixon's latest press conference, attempting to answer grand jury indictment implications in cover-up participation. Presents contradictory aspects of his statements. Details his latest offer of materials to impeachment committee and why unacceptable.

760   March 18, 1974—**Time**, "Examining the Record of That Meeting in March," pp. 10-11.
      Records the different John Dean-H. R. Haldeman-Richard Nixon versions of the March 21, 1973, meeting on hush money, and where the conflicts lie.

761   March 18, 1974—**Time**, "Fairness Factor," p. 71.
      Examines problems now arising in finding impartial juries to sit on the various Watergate trials.

762   March 18, 1974—**Time**, "Question of Zeal," p. 52.
      Comments on criticism of overzealous persecution by the press, along with unethical revelations of supposedly secret grand jury proceedings, made by Joseph Kraft and Howard Simons.

763   March 18, 1974—**Time**, "Watergate: Defining the Law on Deadline," pp. 50-2.
      Examines growing use of lawyer-reporters, especially gaining importance with Watergate coverages. Concentrates on backgrounds and Watergate exclusives of Fred Graham, Carl Stern, and Lesley Oelsner.

764   March 18, 1974—**U.S. News**, "Can Nixon Withstand New Shocks?" pp. 17-19.
      Lists latest problems besetting President Richard Nixon: new indictments, expansion of impeachment inquiry, back taxes, and Republican election losses. Mentions his March 6 news conference. Speculates about what grand jury secret envelope contains.

765 March 18, 1974—**U.S. News**, "President's Own Explanation of Watergate
       'Hush Money'," p. 20.
     Excerpts transcript of President Richard Nixon's March 6, 1974, news
conference.

766 March 20, 1974—**New York Times**.
     Agrees with Senator James Buckley's call for Nixon's resignation.

767 March 21, 1974—**St. Louis Post-Dispatch**.
     Cites Mr. Nixon for intruding on the House inquiry. Compares it with crimi-
nal suspect participating in grand jury proceedings.

768 March 25, 1974—**U.S. News**, "Role of Lawyers in Watergate," pp. 24-5.
     Lists the 11 lawyers convicted or indicted in connection with Watergate, what
the charges are, and bar proceedings now underway concerning them.

769 March 25, 1974—**U.S. News**, "When Nixon Was Asked: 'Would It Not Be
       Better That You Resign?'" p. 30.
     Excerpts portion of President Richard Nixon's speech at the Executive Club
in Chicago in answer to this question.

770 March 29, 1974—**National Review**, "In Like a Lion," George F. Will, p. 364.
     Condemns President Richard Nixon's inflamatory statements about what
evidence he will choose to submit to House Judiciary Committee. Cites current
arguments over what constitutes an impeachable offense.

APRIL 1974

771 April 1974—**Atlantic**, "Judge Who Tried Harder," George V. Higgins,
       pp. 83-106.
     Describes John Mitchell's behavior and testimony on Watergate, background
of Gordon Liddy, 1970 security plan, the prosecution of the Watergate 7 (especially
by Earl Silbert), conduct of the Ervin Committee and its staff, and versions of the
hush money attempts.

772 April 1974—**Discussion**, "Watergate and the Legal Order," pp. 4-6+
     See *Commentary*, January 1974.

773 April 1, 1974—**Newsweek**, "Longest Year . . . The Next Collision," pp. 18-23.
     Briefly reviews Watergate events of the past year, and White House attempts
to garner Republican support for not relinquishing more evidence. Judge Sirica
orders grand jury evidence and sealed letter turned over to impeachment committee.

774 April 1, 1974—**Newsweek**, "What the Tapes Might Show," pp. 20-1.
     Suggest possible contents of 11 additional tapes requested by the House
Judiciary Committee.

775   April 1, 1974—**Time**, "Pressing Hard for the Evidence," pp. 9-12.
    Lists areas subpoenaed evidence pertains to, Judge Sirica's findings for giving grand jury material to the Judiciary Committee, and possible compromises that might be arrived at.

776   April 5, 1974—**Commonweal**, "Europeanization of American Politics," Irving Louis Horowitz, pp. 105-6.
    Contends Watergate has sharpened delineation between the parties, suspended fascist suspension of civil liberties, and increased our isolationism. Wonders at failure of Left to step in with new programs.

777   April 5, 1974—**New York Times**.
    Questions Nixon's disavowal of culpability in his tax errors.

778   April 6, 1974—**New Republic**, "Nixon's Knowledge," Walter Pincus, pp. 16-19.
    Reviews the early Watergate "investigations" and cover-up and Richard Nixon actions and statements about his activities then.

779   April 8, 1974—**Newsweek**, "Buggers' Game," p. 61.
    Reviews article by George V. Higgins in April *Atlantic* on Watergate. Feels he is too derogatory of Ervin Committee and Judge Sirica and too lavish in praise of Earl Silbert. Presents biographical material on Higgins.

780   April 8, 1974—**Newsweek**, "Nixon's Men: Room for Maneuver," pp. 20-1.
    Recounts John Ehrlichman's hiring of a new lawyer, thus dividing his defense from H. R. Haldeman's. Haldeman may also switch from John J. Wilson. Meanwhile, Richard Kleindienst is plea bargaining for a misdemeanor only indictment.

781   April 8, 1974—**U.S. News**, "White House Concession Heads Off Showdown," pp. 26-7.
    Mentions Richard Nixon's complicity with latest subpoenas, turning grand jury report over to Judiciary Committee, and lawyer James St. Clair's request to cross-examine witnesses at impeachment inquiry.

782   April 11, 1974—**Chicago Tribune**.
    Calls for Judiciary Committee to retain its composure in the face of Nixon's delaying tactics, thus forcing him to come around.

783   April 13, 1974—**Washington Post**.
    Condemns the President's stand asserting he alone will determine what evidence to submit. Feels he has no right to interfere in an investigation on himself.

784   April 15, 1974–**Newsday**.
Calls for tax reform, showing that President Nixon, once a tax lawyer, making errors proves the unmanageability of the present system.

785   April 15, 1974–**Time**, "Moving in Committee and Court," pp. 18-19.
Summarizes Judiciary Committee's current attempts to gain materials, conviction of Dwight Chapin, indictments of Ed Reinecke and George Steinbrenner, and testimony of Herbert Kalmbach about the Hughes money.

786   April 18, 1974–**Christian Science Monitor**.
Feels that the loss of Gerald Ford's seat adds to the Republicans' worries over Nixon's standing with the public.

787   April 27, 1974–**New Republic**, "Price of Loyalty," pp. 9-10.
Details the political career of Herbert Porter, including his role in CREEP and the cover-up, and his sentence for lying to the FBI.

788   April 29, 1974–**New Yorker**, "Letter from Washington," Richard H. Rovere, pp. 120-24.
Mentions effects Watergate is finally showing on foreign affairs. Speculates on the possible course impeachment will take. Recapitulates latest election returns.

789   April 29, 1974–**Newsweek**, "New Tape Crop," pp. 30-5.
Lists possible contents of new tapes under subpoena: linking Charles Colson to the cover-up, attempts to involve CIA, hush money, and reactions to John Dean's disclosures.

790   April 29, 1974–**Time**, "Court Calendar," p. 23.
Mentions new tapes requested by Special Prosecutor Leon Jaworski. Lists upcoming trials or sentencing of Ed Reinecke, Dwight Chapin, Jeb Magruder, John Ehrlichman, Charles Colson, Bernard Barker, Eugenio Martinez, and Felipe De Diego.

791   April 29, 1974–**Time**, "Trouble with Lying," pp. 80-1.
Examines the new perjury law under which many Watergaters are being prosecuted. One problem for them will be finding believable character witnesses with knowledge of the veracity of their testimony. Illustrates with Dwight Chapin's trial.

792   April 29, 1974–**U.S. News**, "More Subpoenas, More Problems for Nixon," pp. 23-4.
Mentions new tapes under subpoena by Leon Jaworski and House Judiciary Committee. Mentions previous tape battles. Arguments regarding possible impeachment repeated.

MAY 1974

793   May 1974—**American Bar Association Journal**, "Governmental Secrecy:
          Corruption's Ally," Earl Warren, pp. 550-2.
      Claims the supreme lesson to be learned from Watergate is that governmental
affairs at all levels must be open to public scrutiny and that this is possible only
through stimulation of a free press. Limited allowable secrecy should be set by law
and none beyond that should be countenanced.

794   May 1974—**American Bar Association Journal**, "Politics of Impeachment,"
          Albert Broderick, pp. 554-6+
      Stresses that the Constitution's founding fathers made impeachment a politi-
cal rather than a judicial process by placing it under Congress' domain, and, therefore, citizen input relative to the process is crucial.

795   May 1974—**Current**, "Watergate and American Politics," I. L. Horowitz,
          pp. 3-9.
      See *Commonweal*, April 5, 1974.

796   May 1974—**Current**, "Watergate and Public Morality," Vermont Royster,
          pp. 10-18.
      See *American Scholar,* Spring 1974, "Public Morality: Afterthoughts on
Watergate."

797   May 1974—**Yale Law Journal**, "President, Congress, and the Courts," Raoul
          Berger, pp. 1111-55.
      Lengthy article discusses legal aspects of the Jefferson/Marshall case regarding
subpoenaing the President. Examines the question of whether President or Vice
President can be indicted without impeachment or whether impeachment can come
only on indictable grounds. Presents James St. Clair's anti-impeachment argument.

798   May 2, 1974—**New York Times**.
      In the wake of the tape transcripts, calls for Leon Jaworski to push legally for
full compliance with the subpoenas.

799   May 6, 1974—**Time**, "$100,000 Misunderstanding," pp. 13-14.
      Describes Ervin Committee's investigation of the Howard Hughes-Bebe Rebozo
money fiasco. Goes over Herbert Kalmbach's testimony, in which he claims Rebozo
gave the money to Rose Mary Woods and the two Nixon brothers. Asserts Fred
Buzhardt covered up the money handling.

800   May 6, 1974—**Time**, "President Prepares His Answer," pp. 11-12.
      Presents background to and Richard Nixon's reasons for submitting trans-
cripts instead of tapes themselves to the Judiciary Committee. Also mentions progress in impeachment investigation.

801   May 6, 1974—**U.S. News**, "Why the Tapes Worry Nixon," pp. 26-7.
      Presents an explanation given by an anonymous White House aide about why
Richard Nixon is reluctant to relinquish tapes.

802   May 7, 1974–**Wall Street Journal**.
Condemns type of men President Nixon chose to associate himself and his office with.

803   May 9, 1974–**Chicago Tribune**.
Calls for President Nixon's resignation or impeachment.

804   May 10, 1974–**Los Angeles Times**.
Calls for impeachment and trial of President Nixon, claiming the evidence of the transcripts is sufficient.

805   May 11, 1974–**Business Week**, "Selling of the Transcripts," p. 36.
Describes publishers' efforts to be first out with paperback books of the transcripts.

806   May 11, 1974–**New Republic**, "Doomsday Roar," TRB, p. 4.
Feels the transcripts are the first cataract in the coming deluge. Illustrates how they prove Richard Nixon lied to the public by taking his own remarks out of context.

807   May 11, 1974–**New Republic**, "Excerpts from the Tapes," pp. 13-33.
Excerpts sections of transcripts pertinent to President Nixon's possible involvement in the Watergate cover-up.

808   May 11, 1974–**New Republic**, "Holes in the Story," pp. 5-8.
Examines how many Nixon statements are contradicted by the transcripts and raises further questions of his role in the cover-up.

809   May 11, 1974–**New Republic**, "Tactics," John Osborne, pp. 11-12.
Describes the tactics behind the release of the transcripts. Criticizes press for indulging in allegations and rumors to discredit President Nixon.

810   May 13, 1974–**New Yorker**, "Down the [Adjective Deleted] Road," Calvin
Trillin," p. 37.
Satiric "transcript" of a conversation among a cab driver and his passengers, Watergate style.

811   May 13, 1974–**New Yorker**, "Notes and Comment," p. 31.
Says Richard Nixon, as master of concealment, has stunned the nation with an avalanche of garbled disclosure. Having failed to conceal the evidence of crime, he has launched a campaign to destroy the country's capacity to recognize crime.

812   May 13, 1974–**Newsweek**, "Cover-Up Comes Apart," pp. 39-45.
Briefly reiterates major cover-up problems from March 21, 1973, to John Dean's breaking silence as discussed in the tapes.

813   May 13, 1974–**Newsweek**, "Desperate Gamble for Survival," pp. 17-23.
Discusses devastating effect of release of tape transcripts and Richard Nixon's refusal to release more. Shows the picture of Nixon that the tapes reveal. Contrasts

his public statements with tapes. Release of transcripts a public relations effort doomed to failure. Both Judiciary Committee and Leon Jaworski refuse to accept them in lieu of tapes themselves.

814   May 13, 1974—**Newsweek**, "How Credible Was John Dean," pp. 30-1.
On the basis of the transcripts, John Dean's testimony emerges as surprisingly accurate, despite presidential attempts to discredit him, but Dean did not admit to dealings with Robert Vesco, helping Jeb Magruder to perjure, offering executive clemency, and destroying E. Howard Hunt documents. Dean's own culpability magnified.

815   May 13, 1974—**Newsweek**, "Listening in on Nixon and His Men," pp. 46-92.
Excerpts segments of the tape transcripts from September 15, 1972-April 27, 1973.

816   May 13, 1974—**Newsweek**, "March 21: Hugh-Money Talk," pp. 31-7.
Condenses the March 21, 1973 taped conversation between John Dean and Richard Nixon when Dean first revealed the break-in and the cover-up and discussed the hush money problem.

817   May 13, 1974—**Newsweek**, "'Step Ahead of the Curve'," pp. 38-9.
Summarizes general impressions given by the transcripts of White House interest in public relations aspects of Watergate, attitude toward L. Patrick Gray, attempt to pin Watergate on John Mitchell, and the crumbling of the cover-up.

818   May 13, 1974—**Newsweek**, "Telling the Tape Tale," p. 136.
Records attempts of the press and various publishers to edit and print the White House transcripts as quickly as possible.

819   May 13, 1974—**Newsweek**, "This Is Your President—Warts and All," pp. 18-19.
Portrait of how Richard Nixon appears on the tapes—indecisive, yielding to subordinates. Viewed Watergate as tactical rather than substantial or ethical problem. Excessive paranoia and isolationism.

820   May 13, 1974—**Newsweek**, "(Unintelligible) or (Inaudible)," p. 22.
Speculates on what caused inaudibles and what they might cover up. Ditto for "unrelated" deletions. House Judiciary Committee claims they can clarify some of these and that they are not quite accurate.

821   May 13, 1974—**Newsweek**, "What the President Knew," pp. 24-30.
Transcripts show Richard Nixon may have been aware of cover-up much earlier than he admitted. He himself suggested executive clemency. Coming clean impossible according to John Dean because one domino would cause another to fall.

822   May 13, 1974—**Time**, "Intimate Glimpse of a Private President," pp. 38-9.
Reprints excerpts of transcripts relevant to the personality of the President.

823   May 13, 1974—**Time**, "Letting It All Out," p. 82.
See *Newsweek*, May 13, "Telling the Tape Tale."

824   May 13, 1974—**Time**, "Most Critical Nixon Conversations," pp. 20-39.
Excerpts of the transcripts.

825   May 13, 1974—**Time**, "President Gambles on Going Public," pp. 10-19.
Describes the release of the tape transcripts, why they were released, and encapsulates what they reveal. Judiciary Committee's reaction outlined. New attacks on John Dean's credibility repeated.

826   May 13, 1974—**Time**, "Voters: Nixon Should Go," p. 19.
Reveals results of public opinion poll relating to the transcripts.

827   May 13, 1974—**U.S. News**, "As the Watergate Case Unfolded—," pp. 85-91.
Excerpts various of the tape transcripts.

828   May 13, 1974—**U.S. News**, "Counterattack: Nixon's Bold Gamble," pp. 13-15.
Recapitulates latest Richard Nixon activities: his speech, release of transcripts, and refusal to submit additional tapes. Emphasizes his attempts to discredit John Dean's testimony, and reinforce his own claims of innocence.

829   May 13, 1974—**U.S. News**, "Nixon's Watergate Tapes," pp. 78-82.
Presents James St. Clair's statement issued along with the transcripts pointing out discrepancies between them and John Dean's testimony.

830   May 15, 1974—**Christian Century**, "Waiting for Godot in the Oval Office," pp. 523-4.
Compares transcripts to Theatre of the Absurd dialogue. Condemns Richard Nixon's continuing concern for his "image" rather than welfare of the nation.

831   May 17, 1974—**Commonweal**, "Expletives Removed," pp. 251-2.
Condemns the tapes for their revelations of the pettiness, paranoia, and vindictiveness of the President. Remains stunned that he felt the tapes would help him.

832   May 18, 1974—**America**, "White House Scenarios," pp. 380-1.
Asserts that transcripts are a diversion, yet another White House attempt to manipulate public opinion. Feels they are also being used to neutralize John Dean.

833   May 18, 1974—**Nation**, "'Options' and 'Scenarios': The (Expletive Omitted) Cover-Up," John Lindsay, pp. 617-21.
Excerpts transcripts to show the contrasts between Richard Nixon's public protestations of innocence and his private conversations.

834   May 18, 1974—**Nation**, "Real Richard," Carey McWilliams, pp. 610-12.
Capsulizes transcript evidence proving Richard Nixon's involvement in the cover-up.

835   May 18, 1974—**New Republic**, "Plot Sickens," TRB, p. 4.
      Suggests Watergate as revealed in the transcripts has all the elements of Shakespearian drama and illustrates this theme.

836   May 18, 1974—**New Republic**, "Tapestries," John Osborne, pp. 10-12.
      Describes his recent interview with Fred Buzhardt in which the White House taping system was described in detail to show how gaps legitimately occurred in tapes.

837   May 18, 1974—**Saturday Review/World**, "Watergate on Main Street," Norman Cousins, p. 8.
      The corruption of Watergate is manifested in all levels and areas of everyday life. People barely able to be indignant over national scandals, certainly not local small ones. Upcoming bicentennial should aim toward regeneration, and not fireworks.

838   May 19, 1974—**New York Times Magazine**, "Ends," Archibald Cox, pp. 27-8+
      Attempts to find the causes behind Watergate and suggests reforms.

839   May 19, 1974—**New York Times Magazine**, "Means," Jeb Stuart Magruder, p. 31+
      An excerpt from *An American Life: One Man's Road to Watergate*, detailing how Jeb Magruder first heard about the break-in.

840   May 20, 1974—**New Yorker**, "Notes and Comment," pp. 29-34.
      Records comments of 33 noted people on the transcripts.

841   May 20, 1974—**Time**, "Congress: Black Wednesday," pp. 24-9.
      Records congressional reaction to the transcripts.

842   May 20, 1974—**Time**, "Further Tales from the Transcripts," pp. 29-32.
      Excerpts some of the tape transcripts.

843   May 20, 1974—**Time**, "'Nixon Has Gone Too Far'," pp. 22-3.
      Excerpts eight editorials from major United States papers calling for the first time for Richard Nixon's impeachment or resignation.

844   May 20, 1974—**Time**, "Public: Disillusioned," pp. 18-22.
      Records outraged reactions of longtime press supporters, religious leaders, and general public to the transcripts.

845   May 20, 1974—**Time**, "Richard Nixon's Collapsing Presidency," pp. 15-17.
      Examines reactions to transcripts in Congress, in the press, and Judiciary Committee proceedings. Describes opening of the proceedings. Mentions release of Ervin Committee report, especially regarding the Howard Hughes/Bebe Rebozo money. Repeats evidence regarding 18 minute tape buzz.

846 May 21, 1974—**Wall Street Journal**.
Calls for clear and precise handling of the entire impeachment process so the public will thoroughly understand it.

847 May 23, 1974—**Washington Post**.
Declares President's latest refusal to cooperate now allows everyone to draw whatever inferences they will from his actions.

848 May 24, 1974—**National Review**, "Bunch of Squares," George F. Will, p. 577.
Briefly excerpts some conversations with John Dean that are especially damaging to Richard Nixon.

849 May 24, 1974—**National Review**, "Watergate Blockbuster," pp. 569-70.
Judges the transcript evidence less damning than Richard Nixon's behavior would have indicated. Outlines one interpretation of the March 21, 1973, meeting while mentioning another passage open to dispute.

850 May 25, 1974—**New Republic**, "Watergate Whodunnit," Walter Pincus, pp. 15-17.
Questions why certain of the requested tapes were not transcribed. Speculates about what could be on them. Suggests some taped Richard Nixon statements were made by him deliberately to establish his innocence.

851 May 27, 1974—**Newsweek**, "'Awfully Rough' Game," p. 29.
Excerpts tape transcript in which Richard Nixon threatens to retaliate on *Washington Post* owner by blocking renewal of his TV station's FCC license.

852 May 27, 1974—**Newsweek**, "Big Graffiti," Shana Alexander, p. 35.
Asserts the tape transcripts represent Richard Nixon's attempts at graffiti—no other explanation possible.

853 May 27, 1974—**Time**, "Error of Transcription: 'Bah' or 'Act'?" p. 12.
Points out how easily errors are made in the transcriptions with two widely varying versions of the same conversation.

854 May 27, 1974—**U.S. News**, "Count on the Tapes: Now About 200, and Still Climbing," p. 19.
Lists the figures regarding tapes requested and subpoenaed by Judiciary Committee, those turned over, those transcribed, and those unacknowledged.

JUNE 1974

855 June 1974—**American Bar Association Journal**, "Is Judicial Review of Impeachment Coming?" Daniel A. Rezneck, pp. 681-5.
Suggests the Supreme Court's granting of judicial review in Adam Clayton Powell's exclusion from the House entitles Richard Nixon to the same review, should he be impeached. Presents six lines of argument supporting judicial review.

856   June 1974–**Discussion**, "Judge Who Tried Harder," G. V. Higgins, pp. 30-32.
See *Atlantic*, April 1974.

857   June 1974–**Progressive**, "Get On with It," pp. 5-6.
Reflects on the tape transcripts released by the President and how his lying
and obstructing justice should be impeachable offenses.

858   June 1, 1974–**New Republic**, "Escaping Watergate," John Osborne, pp. 9-11.
Describes flap arising over Richard Nixon's alleged racial slurs deleted from
the transcripts. Speculates about why tape recorders were installed by such a private
president.

859   June 1, 1974–**New Republic**, "Where Truth Lies," pp. 5-6.
Excerpts some of the transcripts dealing with the supposed report on Watergate John Dean was to write, showing how it was never intended to be true, while
President Richard Nixon told Henry Petersen that Dean misled him. More examples
of lies to Petersen given.

860   June 1, 1974–**Vital Speeches**, "Presidential Tapes and Materials," Richard M.
Nixon, pp. 482-6.
Records the April 30, 1974, TV address of President Nixon regarding his sub-
mission of tape transcripts to the Judiciary Committee and the public.

861   June 2, 1974–**St. Louis-Post Dispatch**.
States the Supreme Court's decision to hear tapes case bypassing the lower
court channels is a further indication of the urgency of resolving the Nixon
scandals.

862   June 3, 1974–**Newsweek**, "Heart of the Matter," pp. 25-7.
Recounts impeachment committee reaction to Richard Nixon/John Dean
tape on E. Howard Hunt payoff–although only slightly different from transcripts,
tone of voice, expletives and other deletions alter meaning. No mention on
March 21 dictabelt of investigation Nixon claimed to have initiated that day. ITT
and milk fund to be investigated along with wiretaps, plumbers and taxes.

863   June 3, 1974–**Newsweek**, "Jeb Magruder: Lost Compass," p. 24.
Excerpts some of Jeb Magruder's feelings on what led to his role on Richard
Nixon staff and in cover-up from his upcoming book, *An American Life: One Man's
Road to Watergate*. He says no one in Administration ever questioned that there
would be a cover-up.

864   June 3, 1974–**Newsweek**, "Stonewall Nixon at War," pp. 22-5.
Examines Richard Nixon's refusal to answer subpoenas–possible reasons for
reasons for outcomes. Leon Jaworski has taken the issue to the Supreme Court.
William Saxbe backs his action.

865   June 3, 1974–**Time**, "Boy Scout without a Compass," pp. 14-15.
Reviews Jeb Magruder's career and White House attitudes and actions as
revealed in his book, *An American Life*.

866   June 3, 1974—**Time**, "Nixon: No, No, a Thousand Times, No," pp. 11-13.
       Lists Richard Nixon's grounds for refusing to honor latest subpoenas and
mentions possible consequences of this action. Records tongue-lashing Judge Gesell
gave James St. Clair regarding withholding evidence in the John Ehrlichman/
Charles Colson trial.

867   June 3, 1974—**U.S. News**, "Jeb Magruder: Another Former White House Aide
       Heads for Prison," p. 26.
       Describes Jeb Magruder's political history, his Watergate testimony, and some
excerpts from his book.

868   June 3, 1974—**U.S. News**, "Now It's a Three-Front Battle over the Tapes,"
       pp. 25-7.
       Describes three requests for tapes from: Leon Jaworski, Judge Gesell [Ellsberg
case], and Judiciary Committee and Richard Nixon's responses. Some Judiciary
Committee members' comparison of tapes and transcripts included. Recent opinion
poll results mentioned.

869   June 7, 1974—**National Review**, "Menacing Words," George F. Will, p. 639.
       Discusses passages in Jeb Magruder's book which could prove dangerous to
H. R. Haldeman. Speculates on identity of "Mr. Deep Throat," chief informant to
Carl Bernstein and Bob Woodward, and expresses pleasure in high sales of transcript
books.

870   June 8, 1974—**New Republic**, "Hushabye Boodle," Walter Pincus, pp. 8-9.
       Examines transcript evidence showing President Nixon may have had knowl-
edge of the hush money before the date he admits.

871   June 9, 1974—**New York Times Magazine**, "White House Taped," Emmet John
       Hughes, p. 17+
       Uses the transcripts to deduce the atmosphere and concerns of the Richard
Nixon Administration. Discusses tape-related blunders committed by the White
House.

872   June 10, 1974—**New Yorker**, "Reflections: The Watergate Prosecutions,"
       Richard Harris, pp. 46-63.
       Asserts some legal practices used to bring Watergaters to justice have instead
subverted the law. Discusses plea bargaining in detail. Points out unequal treatment
meted out to Herbert Kalmbach, Herbert Porter, and Richard Kleindienst.

873   June 10, 1974—**Time**, "Nixon's Date with the Supreme Court," pp. 19-25.
       Supreme Court agrees to hear tapes case immediately, bypassing Appeals
Court. Explores reasons for this ruling. Judge Gesell's ruling on White House evidence in Ellsberg burglary trial due. Mentions Judiciary Committee's slowness and
decision not to televise their hearings. Also Henry Petersen illegally offered head of
FBI, John Dean almost left government after '72 elections, and more ITT
investigations.

874   June 10, 1974—**U.S. News,** "Watergate: Fight Against Time—Who's to Blame
         for Delay?" p. 29.
      Explains problems of increasing politicizing of impeachment proceedings as
their timetable lags further and chances increase of it lasting through elections.
Mentions various efforts to speed things up.

875   June 11, 1974—**Christian Science Monitor.**
      Proves that President Nixon's assertions that the investigations are weakening
his presidency are inaccurate.

876   June 12, 1974—**Christian Century,** "Reporters in a Lonely Search for Truth,"
         James M. Wall, pp. 627-8.
      Cites American press for failure to initiate investigation in Watergate,
except for Carl Bernstein and Bob Woodward. Mentions Timothy Crouse's *Boys
on the Bus* concerning press coverage of the '72 campaign.

877   June 17, 1974—**Newsweek,** "Colson: Beat the Devil," pp. 19-27.
      With Charles Colson plea bargaining, speculates about what he could reveal.
Records his "conversion" to Christ and how it influenced him. His testimony may
include ITT and milk fund information.

878   June 17, 1974—**Newsweek,** "Flight from Reality?" pp. 16-19.
      Records latest blows to Richard Nixon: revelation of his name as unindicted
co-conspirator; Charles Colson pleads guilty; Judge Gesell cites Nixon for stone-
walling in John Ehrlichman trial; and Henry Kissinger called regarding wiretapping.

879   June 17, 1974—**Newsweek,** "Price of Plea Bargaining," pp. 27-9.
      Describes plea bargaining of Richard Kleindienst, Charles Colson, Herbert
Porter, Jeb Magruder, and Herbert Kalmbach. Condemns such wide use of it among
Watergaters, especially those with no significantly enlightening testimony.

880   June 17, 1974—**Time,** "California Poll," p. 42.
      Reveals California poll's survey shows public feels press Watergate coverage
has been biased and too massive.

881   June 17, 1974—**Time,** "Four Walls Close In on Nixon," pp. 13-15.
      The week's occurrences: Judiciary Committee to call witnesses, be done by
July 15 for vote; Charles Colson pleads guilty—some of his possible testimony
repeated; Judge Gesell studying possible charges of contempt against President
Nixon; and Nixon's naming as unindicted co-conspirator revealed.

882   June 17, 1974—**Time,** "Is the President Legal Chief?" pp. 55-9.
      Presents pro and con arguments that the President is chief legal executive,
therefore only he can settle dispute with Leon Jaworski, not Supreme Court, since
it is an internal affair. Judge Gesell's difficulties in obtaining White House evidence
enumerated.

883   June 17, 1974—**U.S. News**, "Watergate: Three More Shocks for the President,"
           pp. 24-7.
       Latest bombshells: Charles Colson pleads guilty; grand jury names Richard
Nixon unindicted co-conspirator; and Judge Gesell may cite Nixon for contempt.
Possible Colson testimony outlined. Panel results on 18 minute tape gap repeated.
Richard Kleindienst's sentence mentioned.

884   June 21, 1974—**Science**, "20 June Tape: Critics Fault Logic of Experts'
           Final Report," Nicholas Wade, pp. 1261-2+
       Refutes tape experts' findings about the 18 minute tape hum based on the
newly-released evidence. The theory cited here is a continuation of one proposed
earlier by Allan Bell of Dektor Laboratories.

885   June 22, 1974—**New Republic**, "Somebody's Lying," Walter Pincus, pp. 11-13.
       States President Nixon's refusal to submit more tapes saying live witnesses
should be used instead, is unrealistic because most of them have lied before.
Illustrates point.

886   June 22, 1974—**New Republic**, "Supreme Court and the Watergate Case,"
           Nathan Lewin, pp. 13-16.
       Discusses the arguments to be proposed on both sides to the Supreme Court
in the tapes dispute. Speculates as to court's decision and Richard Nixon's reaction
to it.

887   June 24, 1974—**Newsweek**, "Making a Federal Case of It," pp. 29-33.
       Supreme Court agrees to hear case regarding submission of tapes and legality
of grand jury naming Richard Nixon as unindicted co-conspirator. Enumerates discrepancies in tapes and transcripts.

888   June 24, 1974—**Time**, "Damaging Deletions from the Tapes," pp. 31-2.
       Examines discrepancies between White House and Judiciary Committee trans-
cripts. James St. Clair's attempts to shore up his case for refusal to honor subpoena
reiterated.

889   June 24, 1974—**Time**, "Watergate Bargains: Were They Necessary?" p. 64.
       Criticizes questionable use of plea bargaining in so many Watergate cases and
compares sentencing to that for the average criminal.

890   June 24, 1974—**U.S. News**, "Shift by Nixon Avoids a Showdown with U.S.
           Judge," p. 23.
       Describes compromise reached with Judge Gesell to allow John Ehrlichman to
go through his White House files to be sure there is nothing applicable to his trial
there.

JULY 1974

891   July 1974—**Commentary**, "Did the Press Uncover Watergate?" Edward Jay
           Epstein, pp. 21-4.
       Denies that *Washington Post* reporters Bob Woodward and Carl Bernstein

played major role in revealing the Watergate cover-up, as claimed in their book, *All the President's Men*, and attributes the most significant factfinding to the FBI, federal prosecutors, grand jury, and congressional committees.

892 July 1974—**Current**, *"New Yorker's* Comment," pp. 59-60.
   See *New Yorker*, May 13, 1974, "Notes and Comment."

893 July 1974—**Progressive**, "Coolest Man in the Room," Richard Lipez, p. 50.
   In transcript form, satirizes White House discussion about Gordon Liddy sending an A-bomb to Russia.

894 July 1, 1974—**Newsweek**, "'I Never Questioned Whether It Was Right',"
   p. 16.
   Excerpts Charles Colson's statement at his sentencing.

895 July 1, 1974—**Newsweek**, "Nixon: Fly Now—Pay Later?" pp. 16-18.
   Describes Charles Colson's testimony as indicating President Nixon urged him to spread damaging information on Daniel Ellsberg. Explains how Colson's statements have revved up the impeachment proceedings again.

896 July 1, 1974—**Newsweek**, "Reluctant Inquisitor," p. 26.
   Describes Senator Sam Ervin's questioning of Henry Petersen as to why his Watergate investigation failed to follow up various leaks and leads.

897 July 1, 1974—**Time**, "'We Were Snookered'," p. 16.
   See *Newsweek*, July 1, 1974, "Reluctant Inquisitor."

898 July 1, 1974—**U.S. News**, "Casualties of Watergate—The Record So Far," p. 25.
   Enumerates the indictments and sentences of those tried in Watergate-related matters.

899 July 1, 1974—**U.S. News**, "Furor over Watergate Leaks," pp. 22-5.
   Asserts recent leaks from Judiciary Committee damaging to the President may instead increase partisanship and decrease chances of impeachment. Quotes Archibald Cox against leaks. Lists the latest leaks.

900 July 5, 1974—**National Review**, "Block That Expletive!" S. L. Varnado,
   p. 760+
   Satirizes future presidential tapes, emphasizing clean language.

901 July 7, 1974—**Newsday**.
   Calls for speeding up of campaign reforms.

902 July 8, 1974—**Philadelphia Inquirer**.
   Calls for corrections to the loopholes in the proposed campaign reform bill.

903   July 8, 1974—**Time**, "Colson's Weird Scenario," p. 16.
Presents Charles Colson's allegations the CIA deliberately fouled up the Watergate burglary to bring the Administration to heel. He alleges they even killed Dorothy Hunt.

904   July 8, 1974—**Time**, "Covering Watergate: Success and Backlash," pp. 68-73.
Discusses role of the press in Watergate, including praise and criticism and public opinion, but concentrating primarily on the Bernstein-Woodward investigation.

905   July 8, 1974—**Time**, "Democratic Violations," p. 17.
Lists Ervin Committee's findings on Democratic campaign fund violations in 1972.

906   July 8, 1974—**U.S. News**, "Plea Bargaining: What It Is, Why It's Under Fire in Watergate," pp. 18-21.
Covers pros and cons of plea bargaining both in general and in regard to Watergate. Describes its use in particular with Spiro Agnew and John Dean.

907   July 8, 1974—**Wall Street Journal**.
Hopes the Supreme Court will come to its decision without setting broad precedents, since Special Prosecutor Jaworski's legal basis for suing his employer is cloudy.

908   July 12, 1974—**Science**, "Watergate: 1972 Campaigners Tried to Use R&D Agencies," Deborah Shapley, pp. 124-7.
Reports on a segment of soon-to-be-released Ervin Committee report indicating government funding was to be allocated according to "responsiveness" to the Richard Nixon campaign. Quotes related White House memos.

909   July 13, 1974—**Science News**, "Watergate Spillover in Science Agencies," p. 23.
See *Science*, July 12, 1974.

910   July 15, 1974—**Newsweek**, "Court and the Tapes," pp. 21-4.
Examines the questions to be answered in the Supreme Court's hearing of the tapes case and both sides' points in each area. Speculates as to possible outcome.

911   July 15, 1974—**Newsweek**, "Inside the Watergate Prisons," pp. 26-9.
Describes life at Lompoc and Allenwood prisons for Watergaters Jeb Magruder, Donald Segretti, and Egil Krogh.

912   July 15, 1974—**Newsweek**, "What the CIA Knew," p. 29.
Capsulizes Senator Howard Baker's report on the CIA's role in Watergate, especially their more questionable activities.

913   July 15, 1974—**Time**, "Showdown Before the Justices," pp. 13-16.
Describes the presentation of both sides in the tapes dispute to the Supreme Court. Lists the constitutional issues involved, as well as the pros and cons on both sides.

914   July 15, 1974—**Time**, "Some Foolish Mistakes," p. 19.
See *Newsweek*, July 15, 1974, "What the CIA Knew."

915   July 19, 1974—**National Review**, "Colson Saga: CIA," pp. 794-6.
Presents Miles Copeland's explanation of CIA sponsoring James McCord to deliberately blow the Watergate burglary in order to stymie the White House. This is similar to recent Charles Colson statements.

916   July 19, 1974—**New York Times**.
Reiterates what it feels "Watergate" is all about in terms of presidential abuses, since President Nixon still does not seem to understand it.

917   July 22, 1974—**Newsweek**, "Court's Hard Questions," pp. 48B-49.
Recaps the presentation of Special Prosecutor Leon Jaworski and lawyer James St. Clair before the Supreme Court.

918   July 22, 1974—**Newsweek**, "Encyclopedia of Evidence," pp. 21-5.
Capsulizes pertinent history of Watergate as written in the 4,000+ pages of the Judiciary Committee's report.

919   July 22, 1974—**Newsweek**, "Sam Ervin's Last Harrumph," pp. 47-8.
Examines the Ervin Committee's report, including its recommendations for future legislation, the many Richard Nixon/Bebe Rebozo financial ties, and shady campaign contribution handling by George McGovern, Hubert Humphrey, and Wilbur Mills.

920   July 22, 1974—**Newsweek**, "'Sense of Climax'," pp. 14-18.
Outlines climactic problems facing the President: House Committee's report published in part; discrepancies in White House and congressional transcripts revealed; Supreme Court decision on tapes due; Ervin Committee report out; John Ehrlichman convicted; and another tape lapse disclosed. Describes James St. Clair's cross-examination of John Dean.

921   July 22, 1974—**Newsweek**, "Those Two-Track Tapes," pp. 19-20.
Goes over briefly some of the discrepancies between the White House and Judiciary Committee versions of the tapes.

922   July 22, 1974—**Newsweek**, "Watergate Evidence," pp. 26-46.
Reprints almost the entire text of Judiciary Committee's description of the Watergate evidence from December 2, 1971, to April 30, 1973, and the answering brief by James St. Clair.

923   July 22, 1974—**Time**, "Case of the Doctored Transcripts," pp. 18-20.
Details the discrepancies between the presidential transcripts and the Judiciary Committee's. Recaps the week's impeachment testimony from Fred LaRue, William Bittman, John Mitchell, John Dean, and Henry Petersen.

924 July 22, 1974—**Time**, "Ervin Committee's Last Hurrah," pp. 27-8+
Reviews the Ervin Committee's final report, emphasizing the financial relationships of the Nixons and Bebe Rebozo and suggestions for legislative reform.

925 July 22, 1974—**Time**, "Evidence: Fitting the Pieces Together," pp. 20-5.
Recaps the evidence just published by the Judiciary Committee in detail along with James St. Clair's defense. Contains many quotes from the transcripts and testimony.

926 July 22, 1974—**Time**, "Tide Turns Back Toward Impeachment," p. 9.
Latest developments: Supreme Court hearings under way; John Ehrlichman convicted; Judiciary Committee releases evidence and their transcripts which conflict with Richard Nixon's; and Ervin Committee report released.

927 July 22, 1974—**Time**, "'United States vs. Richard M. Nixon, President, et al.',"
pp. 10-17.
Speculates as to Richard Nixon's actions after Supreme Court reaches its decision. Describes in detail the hearings. Presents major arguments in the case. Includes biographical sketches of the Justices.

928 July 22, 1974—**U.S. News**, "Historic Debate Before Supreme Court," pp. 72-5.
Excerpts the transcript of the Supreme Court's hearing of the tapes issue.

929 July 22, 1974—**U.S. News**, "'Tragic Happenings'—Final Report of Senate
Watergate Committee," pp. 68-70.
Excerpts sections of the Ervin Committee's final report, including legislative recommendations.

930 July 22, 1974—**U.S. News**, "Two Versions of Key Watergate Tapes—A Sampl-
ing," p. 16.
See *Time*, July 22, 1974, "Case of the Doctored Transcripts."

931 July 25, 1974—**Chicago Tribune**.
Praises Supreme Court for its ruling in the tapes case but expresses regret that a ruling on executive privilege had to be forced.

932 July 28, 1974—**Chicago Tribune**.
Praises the Judiciary Committee for framing articles of impeachment that would be approved by the founding fathers and for their bipartisan actions.

933 July 29, 1974—**Newsday**.
Repeats the abuses that have led to the Judiciary Committee's vote on impeachment.

934 July 29, 1974—**Newsweek**, "'Little People Don't Leak'," p. 28.
Excerpts from transcripts of Richard Nixon/Egil Krogh/John Ehrlichman discussion of using polygraphs to determine where leaks were originating.

935   July 29, 1974—**Newsweek**, "'Massacre' to Stonewall," pp. 23-6.
Reviews second installment of Judiciary Committee's report, especially
related to the Saturday Night Massacre, 18 minute tape gap, and release of the
transcripts.

936   July 29, 1974—**Newsweek**, "Rest of the Evidence," p. 22.
Briefly mentions various evidence collected against President Nixon relating
to misuse of IRS and ITT scandal by the House Judiciary Committee.

937   July 29, 1974—**Newsweek**, "Snooping on the 'Enemies'," pp. 26-9.
Reviews White House atmosphere leading to formation of the plumbers, the
Huston Plan, and the plumbers' activities.

938   July 29, 1974—**Newsweek**, "'This Is Hard Work'," pp. 24-5.
Excerpts transcripts relating to Richard Nixon's and Ron Ziegler's reactions on
listening to early Watergate tapes.

939   July 29, 1974—**Time**, "John Dean: The Man with the Scarlet W," pp. 25-6.
In a question and answer format John Dean discusses the turbulence of his
past, why he waited so long to come out with the Watergate story, what he hopes
to do with his future after serving his jail sentence and his relationships with former
White House associates.

940   July 29, 1974—**Time**, "More Evidence: Huge Case for Judgment," pp. 16-20+
Comments on Nixon Administration's attempts to use the IRS and FBI to
harass political opponents, and others of the proposed articles of impeachment
including milking the dairy co-ops and the White House tapes.

941   July 29, 1974—**U.S. News**, "Milk Fund . . . IRS . . . Bugging . . . Highlights of
      the Evidence," pp. 19-21.
Goes over evidence accumulated by Judiciary Committee on IRS use, domestic spying by White House, milk fund, ITT, and Huston Plan. James St. Clair's
defenses presented.

942   July 30, 1974—**Philadelphia Inquirer**.
Condemns Vice President Ford for his recent pro-Nixon statements. Holds
that a potential president should keep his own counsel and seek to unite the
country, not add to divisiveness.

943   July 30, 1974—**Wall Street Journal**.
Suggests impeachment is the wrong way to resolve the quarrel over presidential obedience to subpoenas.

944   July 31, 1974—**St. Louis Post-Dispatch**.
Discusses the importance of Article III in the articles of impeachment in that
it finds the President attempting to destroy the balance of power established by the
Constitution.

AUGUST 1974

945   August 1974–**Esquire**, "Short History of Tape Abuse," Brock Brower,
          pp. 47-9+
Goes into an account of *New York Times* foray into tape when their pencil
reports were challenged and takes us up to the Richard Nixon preoccupation with
this method of recording for posterity.

946   August 2, 1974–**St. Louis Post-Dispatch**.
Condemns the Judiciary Committee for considering the Nixon proposal that
the House impeachment vote be bypassed and proceedings go directly to the Senate.
Urges correct procedures be followed the entire way.

947   August 5, 1974–**Newsweek**, "Good Guys and Bad Guys," Shana Alexander,
          p. 17.
Discusses the fact that the only real "natural villain" to come out of Watergate is Charles Colson, who himself tried to cast Daniel Ellsberg in the role.

948   August 5, 1974–**Newsweek**, "Spotlight on the Tape Vault," pp. 24-5.
Mentions current handling of the tapes under subpoena, along with what evidence they might contain.

949   August 5, 1974–**Newsweek**, "Very Definitive Decision," pp. 23-6.
Discusses the outcome of the Supreme Court's decision, elaborating on their
findings regarding the major points at issue.

950   August 5, 1974–**Time**, "Summer Week in Washington," Hugh Sidey, p. 27.
This was the "week that was": Peter Rodino has his committee well into the
impeachment debate, and Justice Burger is at work in his hilltop citadel deciding
the tapes issue while on the capitol steps 500 praying and fasting kids end their
three day vigil for Richard Nixon.

951   August 5, 1974–**Time**, "Unanimous No to Nixon," p. 20+
Commenting on the Supreme Court's decision against Richard Nixon on the
Watergate tapes, Columbia University Law Professor Abraham Sofaer says that
"executive privilege does not mean executive whim." Mentions other scholars'
feelings that the effect of the decision is likely to place limits on the power of the
presidency.

952   August 5, 1974–**U.S. News**, "Court's Historic Ruling Narrowing President's
          Power," pp. 16-17.
Suggests that far more than Watergate trials is involved in Supreme Court decision on White House tapes, setting bounds on the use of executive privilege and
holding that a president cannot put himself above the law or beyond the courts.

953   August 7, 1974–**Christian Science Monitor**.
Advocates resignation of President Nixon.

954   August 7, 1974—**Philadelphia Inquirer**.
After release of "smoking gun" tape, calls for immediate replacement of the President.

955   August 8, 1974—**Washington Post**.
Calls for impeachment on the basis of abuses of constitutional powers rather than merely obstruction of justice.

956   August 9, 1974—**Denver Post**.
Calls the peaceful departure of ex-President Nixon a triumph for democracy.

957   August 9, 1974—**Los Angeles Times**.
Expresses hope at a newly beginning presidency and praises Nixon for setting the tone for future unity, although he still fails to see his own culpability.

958   August 10, 1974—**New Republic**, "Behind the Eight Ball," pp. 8-9.
Wonders why the President waited until the Supreme Court issued its 8-0 ruling against him to announce that he would comply in all respects. Suggests that when compared to what the court might have said and done the final decision must have brought sighs of relief in San Clemente.

959   August 11, 1974—**New York Times**.
Condemns President Nixon for his resignation, since he once again subverts the constitutional processes. At least President Ford can take the reins of a country that is still intact.

960   August 12, 1974—**Time**, "Stiff Sentences," pp. 21-2.
Reports on harsh sentences given to John Ehrlichman and John Dean for their parts in the Watergate and Daniel Ellsberg cases.

961   August 12, 1974—**U.S. News**, "Watergate Casualties: The List Grows Longer," p. 23.
Comments on former high Republican officials now snared in the Watergate tangle. The big names involved include John Connally, John Dean, John Ehrlichman and Ed Reinecke, and all could draw large fines as well as prison sentences.

962   August 12, 1974—**Wall Street Journal**.
Praises Richard Nixon for a non-bitter resignation. Feels had he made an unfelt confession of guilt it would have been the worst hypocrisy.

963   August 16, 1974—**National Review**, "Watergate Bizarre," D. Keith Mano, pp. 929-30.
Compares Watergate to a play produced by liberals with a script by Richard Nixon and the character half Beckett, half young Arthur Miller.

964   August 19, 1974—**Newsweek**, "All the President's Men," pp. 50-1.
Contains photos, former positions, and current legal status of 28 Watergaters.

965   August 19, 1974—**Newsweek**, "Tapes That Sealed His Doom," pp. 33-4.
Repeats the contents of the "smoking gun" tapes that proved Richard Nixon ordered the cover-up six days after Watergate. Mentions impact they will have on impending cover-up trials.

966   August 19, 1974—**Time**, "Decline and Fall," pp. 53-5.
In a Watergate retrospective *Time* traces the steps from the break-in planning, to the arrest, cover-up plans, reelection in November of 1972, the cracks beginning in the "stone wall," the gathering storm that would implicate nearly all the White House staff and the final debacle that would lead to impeachment had not Richard Nixon resigned.

967   August 19, 1974—**Time**, "Learning from the Tragedy," Henry Steele
         Commager,   p. 88.
Believes that Watergate was a tragedy but not an unmitigated one. Asserts now we ask how it ever happened but in the future we will be proud that we did not allow ourselves to be distracted. We rallied our resources, rejected an attempt to subvert the Constitution and reversed it. Compares the situation with attempts by Aaron Burr to steal the election of 1800, the Civil War and the Great Depression.

968   August 19, 1974—**Time**, "More Blunt Talk in the Oval Office," p. 62.
Partial transcript of Richard Nixon's June 23, 1972 talks with H. R. Haldeman containing the "smoking howitzer" of evidence that was the decisive factor in ending the Nixon presidency, providing fresh insights into Nixon's attitudes towards people and issues.

969   August 19, 1974—**Time**, "Where America Goes Now," pp. 64-7.
Nine leading scholars and observers of the national scene analyze the legacy of Watergate with the thought that Watergate and its climax may have been America's most traumatic political experience of this century.

970   August 19, 1974—**U.S. News**, "Machine vs. Man," Howard Flieger, p. 84.
Flieger editorializes that for the first time a machine became the decisive witness in a contest involving human conduct—and the machine won. Without the tapes, the entire Watergate impeachment affair would have rested on sworn testimony often in conflict.

971   August 19, 1974—**U.S. News**, "Nixon-Haldeman Talks," pp. 69-70.
Relevant excerpts from three conversations that President Nixon referred to in his statement which took place on June 23, 1972, and dealt with FBI investigations that were already underway into the Watergate break-in that happened six days earlier.

972   August 19, 1974—**U.S. News**, "Tapes That Burst Like a Bombshell," p. 68.
On August 5 Richard Nixon, in his fight to stay in office, released transcripts of three conversations held on June 23, 1972, and sought to explain why he ordered a halt to the break-in probe by the FBI. This article gives the complete text of the Nixon address.

973   August 19, 1974—**U.S. News**, "'Third-Rate Burglary' That Toppled a President," pp. 24-6+
Traces what has happened and puts into perspective the fateful sequence of events from the time Frank Wills, security guard, noticed a strip of adhesive across a lock, to the Supreme Court ruling the President must surrender the tapes and documents, up to the resignation of the doomed President.

974   August 21, 1974—**Christian Century**, "After the Fall," James M. Wall, pp. 787-8.
Comments editorially on the contrasting attitudes toward former President Richard Nixon—absolute loyalty and cynical disdain—and that Nixon adds to the polarization by his unique political style that sees only "those who stood with me" and "those who have not been able to give me your support," and can only see Watergate as a "mistake in judgment."

975   August 24, 1974—**New Republic**, "Will We See Him in Court?" Nathan Lewin, pp. 7-9.
Suggests that relief over Richard Nixon resignation produces a sense of generosity that overpowers reason. His supporters see him as a martyr while Leon Jaworski lets it be known that he will wait several weeks before deciding how to proceed. It is suggested that Nixon be treated no more leniently than John Ehrlichman and H. R. Haldeman, and probably more harshly.

APPENDIX

This is a listing of books that might prove of interest to researchers but that were unavailable for examination in time for publication.

Chilling Effect. Lowell Weicker, Jr. New York, Doubleday, 1974. $6.95.

Gemstone: The Left Looks at Watergate. New York, Ramparts, n.d. $10.00; $3.45pa.

Piece of Tape: The Watergate Story, Fact and Fiction. James W. McCord. Washington Media, 1974. $10.00; $3.95pa.

Scandals in the Highest Office. Hope R. Miller. New York, Random, 1973. $6.95.

Watergate: Crime in the Suites. Michael Myerson. New York, International Publishers, 1973. $1.95pa.

Watergate Hearings, Phase One. 8 vols. Dallas, Tex., Leslie Press, 1973.

Watergate: Its Effects on the American Political System. D. C. Saffel. Cambridge, Mass., Winthrop, 1974. $5.95pa.

Year of the Scandal: How the Washington Post Covered Watergate and the Agnew Crisis. Washington, Washington Post, 1973. $3.95pa.

AUTHOR INDEX

TITLE INDEX

SUBJECT AND PERSONAL NAME INDEX

Ehrlichman, John D., 26, 30, 80, 118-119,
129, 133, 135, 137, 145, 149, 157, 159,
162-163, 167-168, 179, 190, 200-201,
203, 207, 210, 217, 219, 226, 249, 252,
260, 265-266, 270, 275, 281, 303, 309,
312, 317-318, 321, 323-324, 326-327,
335, 339, 347-348, 351, 360, 370, 374,
376, 378, 385, 391, 393-394, 397, 423-
424, 434, 436, 452, 462, 468, 480, 532,
538, 563, 603, 605, 612, 626, 629, 642,
652, 682, 695, 706, 714, 716, 721, 724,
728, 737, 743-744, 746, 748, 750, 753,
756, 758-760, 768, 775, 778, 780, 789-
790, 807-809, 812, 815, 817, 821, 824-
825, 828, 833-835, 842, 848, 859-860,
866, 870-871, 873, 878, 881, 885, 887,
890, 892, 898, 908, 919-926, 934, 937,
940-941, 960-961, 964-966, 971, 973,
975
Eisenhower, Dwight D., 499, 513, 666-667
Eldredge, Harold, 43
Electronic Eavesdropping, 59, 173, 501, 593,
612, 627, 682
Ellsberg, Daniel, 44, 190, 248, 313, 652,
838, 895, 937, 940, 947, 966
Ellsberg Break-In, 133, 136, 157, 163, 183,
187, 195, 201, 225, 250, 281, 321, 343,
353, 390-391, 397, 414, 423, 434, 436,
439, 470, 474, 480, 487, 538, 545, 593,
613, 630, 633, 682, 716, 743, 758, 790,
807, 815, 821, 835, 838, 850, 866, 890,
912, 922, 937, 941, 960
Enemies List. See White House Enemies List
Ervin, Sam, 63-64, 77-78, 93, 107, 113,
118-119, 121, 147, 181-182, 190, 211,
217, 269, 273, 285, 316, 318, 352-354,
371, 375, 390, 393, 399, 537, 539, 565,
567, 588, 683, 743, 771, 809, 815, 856,
892, 896-897, 924, 950, 952, 966, 973
Ervin Committee, 65, 103, 182, 186-187,
200, 207-208, 217, 233, 239, 249, 259,
268, 277, 285, 287, 302, 311, 314, 316,
321, 348, 352, 354, 356, 371, 373, 375,
389, 394, 396, 399, 410, 412, 415, 418,
425-426, 449, 462, 465, 479, 485, 488,
493, 496, 506, 514, 517, 546, 561, 603,
631, 668, 674, 703-705, 709-710, 725,
743, 757, 771, 807, 845, 856, 905, 919-
920, 924, 926, 929, 966, 975
  televised hearings, 183, 196, 204, 223,
  241, 248, 256, 261, 267, 285, 289,
  311, 358, 404, 449, 471
Executive Privilege, 84-85, 93, 99, 107,
215, 367, 375, 399, 417, 433, 435, 446,
478, 481, 499, 510, 512, 609, 612, 653,
666, 668-669, 674, 910, 951-952

FBI, 2, 6-7, 12, 30, 42, 45, 50, 79, 107, 130,
179, 195, 200-201, 210, 219, 226, 249,
260, 265-266, 321, 343, 357, 397, 423,
448, 474, 593, 615, 666, 918, 922, 965-
966, 971-973
Failor, Edward, 81
Fairlie, Henry, 42
Farley, James, 840
Fensterwald, Bernard, 217
Fiers, A. Dale, 489, 543
Fiorini, Frank. See Sturgis, Frank
Flanigan, Peter, 45, 674, 968
Fletcher, Joseph, 489, 543
Fletcher, Robert B., 130
Ford, Gerald R., 555, 576-577, 587, 604,
642, 645, 696, 719, 743, 757, 759, 940,
942, 957, 966-967, 969, 975
Ford, Henry, 840
France, William, 48
Frates, William, 881

GAO, 18-19, 21, 182
Galbraith, John Kenneth, 840
Gardner, John, 296, 840
Garment, Leonard, 167, 340, 824, 858, 939
Gavin, James, 840, 940
Gemstone, 163, 265, 270, 281, 973
Geneen, Harold, 862
Grain Fund, 29, 45
Genovese, Eugene, 840
Gerstein, Richard, 19-21, 26, 52
Gesell, Gerhard, 607, 866, 868, 878, 881-
882, 887, 890, 960
Geyer, Alan, 489, 543
Glanzer, Seymour, 219
Gleason, Jack, 566, 571, 649
Goldwater, Barry, 210, 237
Gonzalez, Virgilio, 6-7, 26, 34-35, 60, 67,
107, 486, 514, 595, 652, 724, 747, 922,
964, 966, 973
Goodbody, James, 43
Graff, Henry, 969
Graham, Billy, 290
Graham, Fred, 763
Grand Jury Investigations, 182, 754
Gray, L. Patrick, 7, 30, 42, 49, 82, 86-88,
90-91, 93, 95, 104, 107, 116, 118, 133,
136-137, 157, 167-168, 178-179, 183,
195, 201, 207, 215, 219, 222, 226, 230,
232-233, 260, 266, 275, 312, 321, 343,
391, 397, 414-415, 423-424, 426, 434,
436, 594, 666, 721, 728, 737, 771, 778,
815, 817, 835, 856, 918, 922, 940, 965-
966, 971-973
Gregory, Thomas James, 63-64, 66, 79, 81,
110, 130
Guenther, George, 908
Gurney, Edward, 182, 217, 316, 318, 327,
631, 771, 856

WITHDRAWN